THE PICTS

BY JILL HARDEN

This book explores the lives and achievements of the Picts, and tries to explain in straightforward terms what has been discovered of their story. It also acts as a companion for visitors to Pictish sites and museums.

Towards the end are detailed guides to Historic Scotland's collections of Pictish sculptures at St Vigeans and Meigle. Information on visiting other stones and other museums is given in the final pages.

We invite readers to discover for themselves the various Pictish strongholds, settlements and monastic sites, as well as their sculptures and other artefacts; to marvel at the superb artistry of the craftsmen; and to ponder interpretations of their past.

CONTENTS

Top left: A huntsman from a Pictish grave-marker found at Kirriemuir, Angus.

Left: A human figure carved on a silver-gilt pin found at Golspie, Sutherland.

Opposite: The Maiden Stone, which stands over 3m high near Inverurie, Aberdeenshire.

FOREWORD: TRACES OF THE PICTS

Of all the peoples living in the north of Britain in the first millennium AD, the Picts attract most interest. Their symbols are intriguing. Their jewellery is wonderful. Their sculpture is superb. The power of place at their strongholds is overwhelming. And much of this in lands now considered by many to be remote: from Shetland to Fife, from the Western Isles to Aberdeenshire.

The Picts fought battles with their neighbours, the Gaels of Dál Riata in modern Argyll, and the Britons and Angles to the south. In the 9th century, lands and people were lost to the Northmen (Scandinavians), who first arrived as Viking raiders. But the Pictish legacy was not obliterated.

Who were the Picts? What was it like to live in their times? What did they believe in? Where is the evidence? Some of the answers to these questions lie in fresh interpretations. This book gives a snapshot of the research to date, carried out by archaeologists, art historians, historians and place-name scholars.

A FAST-MOVING FIELD OF STUDY
Pictish studies continue to evolve in significant and exciting ways. Interest in Pictish sculptures dates back at least to the 18th century. Antiquarians have recorded them, academics have studied them, art historians have compared them to works of art produced across the British Isles and beyond. But over the past 10 to 15 years, new windows have been opened on the Picts, allowing us to reassess many of the assumptions made in the past.

Some experts have reinterpreted early historic documentary sources to redraw political maps. Others have reassessed the royal power struggles that affected all Pictish generations. Still others have reviewed place names and proposed different origins, meanings and interpretations of the stories they tell us. Evidence for the Pictish language has been turned on its head. Archaeological excavations have produced much new information, including new insights on both pagan practices and those associated with early-Christian communities.

DOCUMENTARY EVIDENCE
The name Pict comes to us from the Romans. It derives from *picti*, a Latin word meaning 'painted people', first recorded in AD 297. Scholars generally read it as a slang term for the barbarian tribes north of Hadrian's Wall that threatened Roman imperial control, from the late 3rd to the early 5th centuries AD.

However, this name was not used by the tribes themselves. Roman authors are the only contemporary source on this subject. In the late 1st century AD, more than ten tribal names north of the Forth and Clyde are recorded in Latin. It seems likely that there were many more.

Below right: A decorative silver pin, more than 15cm long and used to fasten a cloak. It was found at Gaulcross near Banff in Aberdeenshire.

Below: Dundurn near St Fillans, Perthshire, site of a Pictish hillfort.

There is increasing evidence for the extent of literacy among the Picts, but aside from a list of kings, all surviving Pictish texts take the form of short inscriptions on carved stones and other objects. When it comes to documentary evidence, we are therefore almost totally dependent on what the Picts' neighbours wrote about them.

Battles, warlords and even peasants are mentioned in chronicles and biographies, including those written in Ireland, Anglian Northumbria and further afield. Abbot Adomnán of Iona, the late-7th-century biographer of St Columba, refers to contact with the Picts. A few decades later, the Northumbrian monk Bede wrote a history of the English people, which describes Northumbrian encounters with the Picts. Other contemporary sources exist too, but all have to be read with the original audience and the authors' intentions in mind.

OTHER SOURCES

Place names can be revealing, although their history is complex. For example, the elements 'pit' or 'pett' relate to farms or estates taken over by Gaelic speakers who were familiar with Pictish words. Archaeology has also contributed much new knowledge. This includes insights into the kinds of home that people built and lived in; what they ate, made and used; how communities and larger groups functioned. Archaeologists may discover signs of contact with other people, such as trade, battles or travel. Their work also highlights changes through time, as reflected in building styles, the form or decoration of objects, or changing patterns of settlement across the landscape.

Portmahomack in Easter Ross, Rhynie in Aberdeenshire and Forteviot in Perthshire are the subject of integrated research programmes. However, all too few Pictish sites have been investigated and there are vast gaps in knowledge. Known Pictish strongholds, burial places, religious centres and settlement sites are rare – not because they don't exist but because they have not yet been identified.

Above: The cross-slab at Dunfallandy, Pitlochry, featuring wild beasts and angels around an elaborately carved cross.

Pictish sites have usually been discovered by chance; however, aerial photography has revealed evidence of numerous uninvestigated sites that may be Pictish.

The greatest transformation of the Pictish era, the conversion to Christianity, has been the subject of surprisingly few research projects. One particularly important breakthrough is the work at Portmahomack, a major monastic complex north of the Moray Firth. Excavations on the Isle of May in the Firth of Forth have also revealed an early-Christian monastic site, at the interface between Pictish and Anglian territories. But these were large establishments, and not necessarily related to conversion as such. More typical sites might be represented by single cross-slabs. At these sites and others, many more discoveries may yet be made.

INTRODUCTION

Left: Female rider from a hunting scene on the cross-slab found at Hilton of Cadboll, Easter Ross.

The Picts are a fascinating people. They lived north of the Forth and Clyde, during a time that experts once called the Dark Ages, now referred to as the early-historic or early-medieval period. Studies of available sources from all possible perspectives have ensured that the period is no longer so dark or mystifying. It is now recognised as a complex, vibrant time, and an era of change.

The Picts were not incomers. They were descendants of the native Iron-Age peoples of the country. Some of their ancestors had agreed treaties with leaders of Roman Britain. Others had joined with neighbouring tribes and raided the lands south of Hadrian's Wall in what is now northern England.

The power of Pictish chiefs was founded on rich agricultural lands and the people who farmed them. The Picts competed between themselves for control of these lands, seaways and resources. Over time it seems that the number of independent warlords decreased. Presumably overlords agreed to come together in support of individual regional kings, in return for greater riches as well as security.

At the same time, the Irish, British and Angles began to introduce Christianity to the Pictish aristocracy and their kindred. From the mid-6th century onwards, for instance, Irish monks established small monasteries and hermitages along the west coast. Some were also established in the east. One theory is that the Picts carved and erected stones bearing Pictish symbols in reaction to this new religion.

Pictish symbol stones are the best-known artistic achievements of the 6th and 7th centuries. But Pictish craftsmen also produced very high-quality, personal status symbols for their leaders, in the form of jewellery. Very little of this solid silver jewellery has survived, but that which has is impressive.

In time, the kings and overlords decided to work with the power of the Christian faith rather than against it. A powerful liaison between church and kingship gradually emerged, a process that had already taken place across much of Europe. Cultures were changing; concepts and artistic styles were being exchanged. The Pictish response to these developments was remarkably creative. This can be particularly appreciated in the carved stones the Picts produced in the 8th and 9th centuries, notably large cross-slabs, carved in relief with

Christian imagery, as well as animals, secular figures and abstract designs. Pictish kings and nobility also supported the establishment of new and sometimes major religious centres, as a wider range of surviving stone monuments testifies.

But these were not peaceful times. There are many contemporary references to conflicts. And in the 9th century the peoples of the British Isles were thrown into even more turmoil by sustained Viking raids. During this period, life must have been very insecure, with the taking of slaves and the plunder of food and portable wealth. These catastrophes led to further changes in society. Eventually, lands in the far north and west that were originally Pictish came under Norse rule.

Changes are also evident across the lands that were still ruled by Pictish kings. Pictish symbols ceased to be relevant by the middle of the 9th century. By the end of the 11th century, the Pictish language had died out, the result of a range of factors, such as acceptance of Gaelic-speaking refugees fleeing Viking raids and the impact of incursions by these Northmen on the Picts themselves.

However, while the name 'Pict' disappears from documentary sources in the early 10th century, it is clear that the people remained and adapted to new social, economic and political times. Their distinctive identity was ultimately subsumed within the newly defined kingdom of Alba.

Above: The reverse of the cross-slab at Elgin Cathedral in Moray, showing Pictish symbols and a hunting scene.

A NOTE ON THE ILLUSTRATIONS

A number of illustrators have contributed to this book.

WILLIE RODGER is a painter and printmaker. He was invited to produce a series of 11 lino-cut prints, based closely on human figures carved on specific Pictish stones. These have been used to introduce the theme of each chapter.

IAN G. SCOTT is a leading illustrator of carved stones. Two illustrations were commissioned from him for this book, including a coloured rendition of the Hilton of Cadboll stone. Some of his pre-existing illustrations have also been used.

STEPHEN CONLIN specialises in highly detailed illustrations of architectural and/or historical subjects. He has produced two new illustrations for this book, including a reconstruction of Burghead fort.

CHRIS BROWN has illustrated many books with historical themes. For this book he has produced a coloured version of an earlier illustration showing the Pictish settlement at Easter Kinnear.

DAVID SIMON is a long-standing contributor to Historic Scotland publications. His illustrations in this book were commissioned by the Western Isles Council, to which we are grateful for permission to reprint them here.

SYMBOLS AND STONES

The Picts are renowned today for their skilful carvings on stones, particularly a range of unique designs – so-called symbols – found repeated on many of their stones. The symbols were once considered inexplicable, but theories have now been developed which help explain their meaning.

Pictish symbols have been found in very simple forms, but are better known as refined and elaborate motifs, on impressively carved sculptures commissioned by local chiefs or regional overlords. What is remarkable is how widely the same symbols are used.

The monuments on which they occur take different forms. Most examples are to be found incised on the 200 or so large, flat-faced boulders that have been recorded north of the Forth. Sometimes called Class I stones, these appear to have been carved during the 6th and 7th centuries AD, occasionally using pre-existing standing stones.

Above: A man depicted on the cross-slab found at Golspie brandishes a knife and an axe.

Opposite: The roadside stone at Aberlemno, Angus, featuring incised symbols: serpent, double-disc and Z-rod; mirror and comb.

Right: A disc about 5cm in diameter, found at Eswick in Shetland. It is marked with a double-disc and Z-rod.

The stones were set up at chosen places in the landscape, some being sited for maximum visibility.

From the 8th century, the symbols appear – in relief and in more ornate forms – on dressed-stone monuments also bearing Christian imagery, known as cross-slabs. These are sometimes called Class II stones. In both cases, the symbols were carved using fine punches, mallets and smoothing stones.

The purely Pictish 'messages' are generally expressed by pairs of symbols, largely undecipherable to us. A statement is made through the choice of symbols, from a repertoire of around 40. There are perfect circles, crescents and rectangles and wild animals such as a stag or salmon, caught in profile. There are also more abstract forms, such as the so-called flower symbol.

SYMBOLS MADE SIMPLE

Top, left to right: Double-disc and Z-rod; crescent and V-rod; Pictish beast.

Centre, left to right: Salmon; eagle; serpent and Z-rod.

Bottom, left to right: Mirror and comb; 'flower'; 'tuning fork'.

Experts have identified about 40 motifs which are known as Pictish symbols (as distinct from other figures that appear on some Pictish carvings). These were incised or carved on stones throughout the regions occupied by the Picts, and on certain Pictish artefacts that have survived, including jewellery. They can be split into three main groups: abstract motifs, everyday objects and animals.

Some symbols appear much more frequently than others; and some are more common in particular parts of the country. These variations provide tantalising glimpses of the choices made by the Picts when incising their symbol stones.

There are 20 or so abstract symbols. These can be sub-divided into designs based on circles, rectangles, crescents and variants of these forms. The two abstract symbols that appear most frequently are known as the **double-disc and Z-rod** and the **crescent and V-rod**.

Then there are a handful of Pictish symbols which appear to represent everyday objects, such as the **mirror and comb** and the **hammer and anvil**.

The animal symbols, such as the **boar** and **wolf**, attract much attention as they are highly naturalistic. But the repertoire is limited – there are fewer than 10 which appear alongside other symbols. The **eagle**, **salmon** and **snake** appear frequently, but most common of all is the **Pictish beast**. This intriguing figure is clearly swimming. Is it a porpoise, a dolphin or a creature of myth?

Although Pictish symbols usually appear in pairs, a few have only been found on their own. These include the **bear** and the **bull**. Other single animals have been found on stones that are incomplete. In these cases, it is difficult to tell whether they were intended to appear alone or as part of a pair.

The range of abstract and animal symbols, as well as representations of certain objects, is quite specific. Most were carved in pairs, generally placed one above the other, sometimes with a mirror or mirror and comb beneath them. Occasionally a stone is carved with two different pairs on the same side, or on both faces. There are even a couple of examples where the carver turned the stone upside down before carving a new symbol pair. This shows that incised stones could have multiple lives, reworked at different times. In this way, the addition of new symbols could bring new meanings to the monument.

In many cases, the carving of these symbols is a superb artistic achievement, often depicted with an elegant economy of line. The abstract symbols may be filled with attractive designs such as tight scrolls and arcs, while the animal symbols have scrolls and lines to define muscles, feathers and even scales.

The use of symbols is now generally seen as the Pictish response to literacy, at a time when the written word was emerging as an important apparatus of power. As we shall see in the next chapter, one strong possibility is that the combinations of symbols represent the names of specific individuals in a form of writing. The suggestion that they recorded tribal lineages or marital agreements is no longer generally accepted.

There are also a number of Pictish carvings which are probably contemporary but do not feature Pictish symbols – small, cross-marked stones. These are thought to be grave-markers, but are impossible to date precisely unless associated with a burial. They probably reflect Christian activity in the 6th and 7th centuries.

The increasing influence of Christianity from the late 7th century onwards – with the patronage of local or regional potentates – saw sculptors adopt new, more complex carving techniques and new forms of monument.

Right: An elegant depiction of a Pictish beast above a double disc and Z-rod on a symbol stone at Dyce, near Aberdeen.

Left: The symbol stone at Abernethy round-tower, featuring a hammer and anvil separated by a 'tuning fork' above a crescent and V-rod.

The cross and its associated Christian imagery is at their heart, but there was obviously still a need to include Pictish symbols as well.

Over 70 large cross-slabs and smaller grave-markers are now known. Some of the monuments have not survived, but more than 40 of those that have incorporate pairs of symbols, usually on the non-cross side. A single symbol survives on a further 10 cross-slabs.

Integrating their own artistic styles with influences from Ireland, Northumbria and the Continent, the Picts began to create sculptures carved in relief on both sides of large slabs of dressed stone. Alongside Christian imagery, they carved religious or secular leaders, beasts or demons and other subjects, as well as traditional symbol pairs. On these finely wrought stones, the symbols are generally filled with spirals, interlace and geometric patterns. These cross-slabs are magnificent celebrations of craftsmanship.

Other figures are also to be found on the large Pictish cross-slabs. In the past, a few of these, such as the centaur and lion, have been mistaken for Pictish symbols. It is now recognised that they are actually Christian symbols, adapted by Pictish craftsmen. The pair of hippocamps – part horse, part fish – on the front of the churchyard slab at Aberlemno in Angus are delightful Christian motifs. The Rodney Stone at Brodie in Moray has a similar pair but they are hybrids and different in style. These creatures are heavy and solid, like the Pictish symbols carved below them. Similar hybrids also feature on the cross-face of the Maiden Stone near Inverurie, Aberdeenshire, and the stone at Logierait in Perthshire.

Top left: Two intertwined hippocamps (part horse, part fish) carved on the Aberlemno churchyard stone.

Top right: A very different treatment of hippocamps on the Rodney Stone, Brodie.

WERE THE STONES COLOURED?

Archaeological discoveries rarely give an indication of the use of colour in the past. Although prehistoric textiles and objects survive in hues of brown today, dyes and pigments must have been used. Pictish jewellery reflects a love of colour, decorated as it is with gold and amber, blue glass and red enamel. A great range of colours can also be seen in the illustrated manuscripts of the period.

There is no reason to think that the Picts did not apply colour to their incised symbols, picking out their shapes as the metalworker did on the silver plaques found at Norrie's Law, Fife (see page 21). And some of the sculptured cross-slabs could surely have been painted masterpieces, mimicking the splendour of the colourful, ornate and shiny metalwork which clearly provided inspiration to the sculptors.

This artist's impression shows part of the cross-slab from Hilton of Cadboll in Easter Ross in colours used during this period, allowing us an idea of how these sculptured masterpieces might have looked.

I·G·S·2010

SINGLE SYMBOLS

The simplest Pictish symbols are those that appear either among a jumble of others on rock-faces, inside caves, or singly on small slabs and carved artefacts. Those on cave walls are not easily accessible and are therefore least well known. They are found at only a few places across the country. Individual symbols have been found incised into the walls of caves at East Wemyss in Fife (see page 42) and Covesea in Moray. Other single symbols have been found, but their original context is unknown. For instance, we do not know where the small stone slabs from Dunnicaer, near Dunnottar in Aberdeenshire, were set, but this rock-stack must have been a place of special significance.

The best known of the small slabs are the six surviving bull symbol stones from Burghead, Moray, once the site of a mighty fort (see page 25). But there are others. For example, a slab found during excavations of a settlement at Scatness, Shetland is incised with a bear – a highly naturalistic, lumbering form. These small slabs could not have been erected in the ground. If they were to be seen they must have been set on a slope, or in a wall. Other single animals appear on larger stones that were once standing, but they are equally rare. We can only guess at their use.

Individual human figures are equally difficult to explain. Only six have been found so far: they may represent important or legendary figures. We do not know why they were carved and erected in the landscape. But occasionally, as at Rhynie, there is a highly intriguing relationship between the stones and their surroundings (see page 14).

These small symbols and single animal or human figures are remarkable. There are not many of them, they have not been found in consistent locations, and the messages they portray are almost impossible to interpret. Groups of early symbols found in caves might be associated with traditional rites of passage. The bull could be the symbol of Burghead, or may reflect the identity of the people of the region. The human figures from Rhynie might represent mythological men or specific leaders. But these carvings might also have been reminders of the powers associated with the place rather than just of those represented.

Below: The incised bear found during excavations at Scatness in Shetland, on a small slab just 35cm wide.

This page: The Craw Stane, standing above Rhynie, Aberdeenshire, in what may be its original position.

LOCATING STONES

Around 200 stones have been found incised with Pictish symbols, but with no relief carving and no Christian imagery. Some survive as lone monuments, while others form clusters. Only a few seem to be in their original setting, but their individual life-histories provide a fascinating insight into attitudes towards such carved stones, from Pictish times right up to the present. Many were broken up for use in drystane dykes or building works – this was the fate of the pieces from Ardross in Easter Ross. Sometimes stones have been moved only 100 metres or so to the edge of a field. Many stones are still associated with the church or graveyard where they

were found (like those at Dyce, near Aberdeen) but others were moved there for safekeeping. Landowners sometimes transported them to the grounds of a country house, but the majority are looked after in museums – on-site, local, regional or national.

Symbol stones have occasionally been found during archaeological excavations. Examples include the stones found at the settlement site at Pool on Sanday, Orkney, and one at the burial mound at Garbeg, above Loch Ness. Others have been found while ploughing fields, like those from Easterton of Roseisle in Moray and Dunrobin in Sutherland.

THE REVELATION OF RHYNIE

Today, Rhynie is an unassuming Aberdeenshire village nestling above a loop of the Water of Bogie. But the eight incised stones that have been found here suggest it was a significant place in Pictish times.

Two stones each have a single human figure carved on them. The other six are typical symbol stones, each bearing a pair of symbols. This high concentration of incised Pictish symbols and single figures is unique to Rhynie.

Three of the stones were found in the village. Two more were found at the site of St Luag's Church, some 500m south of the settlement, down by the river. Another, known as the Craw Stane, still stands high above the site of the church, at the crest of the steep slope (see page 13). The other two stones were found while ploughing nearby. One is the 'Rhynie Man': a grim, threatening figure stomping to the right, brandishing a battle-axe.

Research into this unusual early-historic landscape has revealed that the Craw Stane stands at the inner entrance to a stronghold of unknown date. Now invisible, it once had two ditched ramparts and an outer wooden palisade with an annexe to the west. Other prehistoric sites in the vicinity include Tap O' Noth, a prominent landmark and one of the largest vitrified forts in the country. It may be that the area, already marked by earlier features, was further defined by symbols and human figures on standing stones. They must reflect its importance as a special place of Pictish power or ritual.

Above: The 'Rhynie Man', now displayed at the offices of Aberdeenshire Council in Aberdeen.

Below: Three of the other incised stones found at Rhynie.

Right: Artist's impression of a Pictish burial cairn.

Below right: The Clach Biorach symbol stone at Edderton, Easter Ross, a prehistoric standing stone later incised with Pictish symbols and still in its original position.

There are various interpretations as to why the symbol stones were set up in the landscape. They may have been placed at boundaries between Pictish centres to confirm control and identity, on routeways, or at prehistoric sites to re-state traditions of power and belief. In situ examples of prehistoric standing stones incised with Pictish symbols include Clach Biorach at Edderton, Easter Ross, and Nether Corskie in Aberdeenshire, and probably also the example at Aberlemno roadside. Some are located above river confluences: they might mark long-established places for gatherings and hence the subsequent link to Christian sites of worship. A few seem to be associated with strongholds or places of ritual. Occasionally they relate to Pictish burials (as at Tillytarmont, Aberdeenshire, and Inchyra, Perthshire), but often they were recovered in the 19th or 20th centuries without further investigation, and it is difficult to determine whether they were originally grave-markers.

Pictish symbol stones may have had a variety of functions, but most experts believe the symbols themselves were intended to affirm connections to specific individuals, such as ancestors or local overlords, and to strengthen connections between the families of these individuals and the land where they were placed. Perhaps statements associated with identity were a response to changing times, a reaction against gradual attempts to introduce new beliefs.

ALLEN AND ANDERSON

In 1903 the major work *The Early Christian Monuments of Scotland* was published. Its first part was a review of the known sites and artefacts of the period, written by Joseph Anderson, the Keeper of the National Museum of Antiquities of Scotland. The remainder was written by J. Romilly Allen, who undertook years of research to produce it.

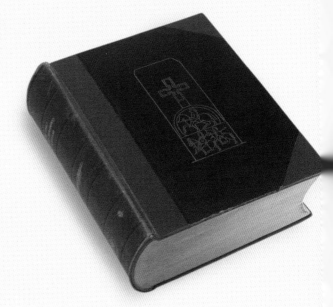

Joseph Anderson was born in St Vigeans and gained early inspiration from the carved stones in its graveyard. Romily Allen was a successful civil engineer who turned, mid-life, to the scientific study of the sculptured stones of Scotland and further afield. His contribution to the volume is a comprehensive analysis of all of the symbols, interlace, geometric patterns and spirals that appear on the stones. Even today, this is still the main reference for the designs. The book also includes a full catalogue of all of the sculpture then known, with drawings or photos, descriptions and measurements. The details are invaluable.

Allen and Anderson devised a classification system for Pictish stones, dividing them into three categories. 'Class I' comprised unshaped stones incised with Pictish symbols, but lacking Christian imagery. 'Class II' stones were dressed slabs carved with crosses and other Christian motifs, along with Pictish symbols. 'Class III' was used to describe Pictish Christian monuments with no Pictish symbols.

Most experts now consider this classification system too rigid. Nonetheless Allen and Anderson's contribution to our understanding of the Pictish and other stones of Scotland cannot be overestimated. Although published over 100 years ago, their book is still one of the most important sources for those studying the sculptured stones of the period.

SYMBOLS ELSEWHERE

Aside from the incised stones, Pictish symbols are also inscribed on a few seemingly everyday objects. Single symbols have been found on items made of stone and bone during excavations in the Western Isles, Orkney and Shetland. Clearly, other objects made from bone, leather and wood – materials that rarely survive – may also have been carved with Pictish symbols. For example, incised or painted symbols may have appeared on architectural timbers, on clothing or bags, on tools or horse gear.

Right: The reverse side of the 5cm-diameter disc found at Eswick, Shetland (see page 7). This side is incised with a triskele, a popular motif of the first millennium, used by many cultures including the Picts.

Jewellery produced by the Picts during the 6th and 7th centuries sometimes features symbols. Examples include the pair of leaf-shaped silver plaques found at Norrie's Law and the silver chain found at Whitecleugh, Lanarkshire.

All of these objects reflect the way in which Pictish symbols were used. They and the surviving stones are a magnificent legacy from the first millennium AD. They form an intriguing resource, aspects of which will remain an enigma.

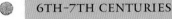

CARVING AND CREATIVITY

● **5TH–7TH CENTURIES**
Symbols carved on small slabs and occasionally in caves.

● **6TH–7TH CENTURIES**
Silver objects produced, a few incised with symbols.

Incised symbol stones erected, a few with ogham inscriptions, as well as simple cross-marked stones.

● **LATER 7TH–9TH CENTURIES**
Cross-slabs carved in relief and erected, a few with ogham or Roman alphabet inscriptions, as well as simple cross-marked stones.

● **8TH–9TH CENTURIES**
Large silver brooches produced as status symbols.

● **LATER 8TH CENTURY**
St Andrews Sarcophagus created.

● **AROUND 800**
A hoard of silver objects hidden on St Ninian's Isle, Shetland.

● **LATER 8TH–9TH CENTURIES AND BEYOND**
Slender, tall cross-slabs and free-standing crosses carved in relief erected, a few with Roman alphabet inscriptions.

● **AROUND 820**
Dupplin Cross created.

● **AROUND 900**
Sueno's Stone erected.

Left: A silver chain featuring a terminal carved with Pictish symbols, found at Whitecleugh, South Lanarkshire.

TRANSLATING SCRIPTS

'In the province of the Picts a certain peasant… listened to and learned through an interpreter the word of life preached by the holy man, St Columba.'

– Adomnán, *Life of Saint Columba*, late 7th century

The Picts spoke a Brittonic language, similar to Welsh and Cornish. Pictish has not survived as a spoken tongue; however, traces of it can still be detected.

In the first millennium BC, the common root of the native languages spoken across the British Isles was Celtic. But these languages evolved with time. In Ireland and the far west of Scotland, Celtic developed into Gaelic. Linguists refer to the various strands of this language as Q-Celtic. In other regions, P-Celtic (or Brittonic) languages developed, including Pictish.

Pictish gradually died out during the 10th and 11th centuries, and Gaelic became the everyday language of former Pictish regions. However, place names composed of Brittonic elements can still be found across the north and east of modern Scotland. Examples include Pluscarden, Aberfeldy, Lendrick, Fintry and Pittenweem.

Right: A spindle whorl, used as a weight in spinning yarn. Found at Buckquoy, Orkney, it features an ogham inscription.

Opposite: An ogham inscription on the stone found at Brandsbutt, Aberdeenshire.

Above: A monk holding a book, depicted on the cross-slab from Aldbar Chapel, near Brechin, Angus.

Experts believe the place-name element 'carden' – meaning either 'wood' or 'enclosure' – is probably specifically Pictish, as 'carden' is not recorded elsewhere. It exists today in places like Urquhart and Kincardine. However, other elements, like 'aber', 'lanerc' and 'tref' are found much further afield, into Wales and Cornwall. They must be Brittonic elements that were used by Pictish speakers in north and east Scotland.

But the most frequent Pictish place-name element 'pit' – meaning piece or portion of land – is nearly always linked to a Gaelic personal name, as in Pittodrie, Pitmedden and Pityoulish. This indicates that these 'pit' place names were created by Gaelic speakers familiar with Pictish, perhaps in the 10th and 11th centuries.

Further north and west, elements of the Pictish language are practically invisible. Norse settlers in Shetland, Orkney and Caithness obliterated Pictish, while in the Western Isles, Skye and the north-west mainland, Pictish was swamped by Norse and then Gaelic.

READING BETWEEN THE LINES: THE OGHAM ALPHABET

Ogham is a form of writing that originated in Ireland and was later adopted by the Picts. Twenty different 'letters' were formed from straight lines: between one and five horizontal or diagonal lines attached to a single vertical line. Ogham was read from bottom to top.

Right: A guide to the way letters are formed in ogham.

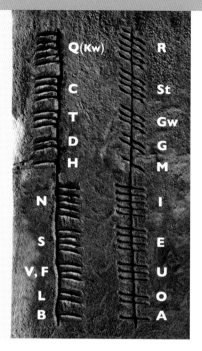

WRITING

Like other peoples of post-Roman Britain, the Picts carved inscriptions in stone. In addition to their symbols – their unique writing system – the Picts also adopted the Irish ogham script and the Roman alphabet.

This practice was certainly inspired by Roman inscriptions and coinage. It represented power and privilege. Inscriptions could act as permanent public records that provided lasting statements of ownership or authority, despite the fact that relatively few people could read.

Fewer than 40 ogham inscriptions have survived in northern Britain and only a small number can be translated. A few are in Gaelic, others are in Pictish. They provide a glimpse of Pictish personal names, scribed into symbol stones and Christian cross-slabs. One example is 'Ethernan', part of the long ogham inscription around the edge of the Rodney Stone cross-slab. Other statements in ogham are inscribed across the faces of symbol stones, like that from Ackergill, Caithness.

These are monumental statements relating to individuals. But occasionally Pictish ogham is found applied to everyday objects, like a stone spindle whorl or a bone handle. This need not imply that writing and reading ogham was common across communities, more that its use was a powerful symbol of ownership or of links with the elite.

Top right: This symbol stone from Ackergill, Caithness, features an inscription in ogham.

Right: The inscription on the Drosten Stone at St Vigeans, Angus, is written in Roman characters.

The Roman alphabet was also used. Those Picts who became monks learned to recite Latin and some must have become proficient at reading and writing. From the late 7th century, the names of Pictish kings were compiled in a list using the Roman alphabet. The original manuscripts have been lost, but this means of recording the names of political and religious leaders, or significant events, must have been important to the Pictish overlords during the 8th and 9th centuries, for they continued the tradition.

There are a few inscriptions carved on stone monuments that include Pictish personal names. For instance, named individuals are recorded in Latin on both the Dupplin Cross, now at Dunning in Perthshire, and one of the cross-slabs from Portmahomack.

Symbols, ogham and Roman letters were used side-by-side and sometimes on the same monument for well over 300 years. However, as societies changed, so their kings and clerics concentrated on a form of writing that could cross boundaries. The Roman alphabet that we use was increasingly adopted, while ogham and Pictish symbols died out by the 10th century.

Right: A knife found at Gurness on the Orkney mainland features an ogham inscription on its bone handle.

Above right: The pair of enamelled silver plaques, each 9cm long, found at Norrie's Law in Fife. Each features the same pair of symbols.

SYMBOLS

Some experts believe that the symbols were another writing system – however, this does not mean that each symbol is part of an alphabet. As we have seen, Pictish symbols almost always appear in pairs, usually one above the other. Close study of these pairings suggests that they may be a form of personal identification, designed to name a specific individual – whether represented on a large standing stone, a magnificent item of jewellery, or a small bone pin.

Symbol pairs on Pictish cross-slabs occasionally seem to identify certain individuals. One example is the Dunfallandy stone at Pitlochry, Perthshire, where three human figures are each accompanied by symbols. The fact that certain pairings occur more frequently than others need not invalidate the theory that together the symbols form a writing system. Names were regularly passed down through generations, as in the case of the Scottish kings James I to James VI.

Those symbol stones that survive in situ are generally interpreted as relating that landscape to a specific individual, and by implication with that person's kindred group. Across the British Isles, inscribed monuments of this period usually state the facts: 'This was erected by …', 'This belongs to …', or 'Here lies …'. The incised Pictish symbols could well have served a similar function.

LORDSHIP AND KINGSHIP

Pictish society developed from a system of numerous rival warlords to a more streamlined structure, with fewer kings recognised by greater numbers. There were frequent upheavals, but by the early 10th century, a powerful and long-lasting Gaelic-speaking dynasty had emerged from the Pictish heritage of previous centuries.

The last 50 years of Roman military presence south of Hadrian's Wall was a period of turmoil. Roman historians recorded major incursions from AD 367 by an alliance of barbarian peoples – including Franks and Saxons from across the North Sea, Scotti from the west, and Picti. The attacks seem to have continued until AD 384 when these raiders were eventually seen off, for a while at least.

So who were these 4th-century Picti? Nowadays they are thought of as professional warbands, living off the booty taken during raids on farms and villages. Between raids they returned home, to the various kingdoms north of Hadrian's Wall.

By the 6th century the Romans had left, and the territorial divisions in place by then are named in 8th-century sources. South of the Forth and Clyde were the kingdoms of Dumbarton, the Gododdin,

Rheged and Bernicia. To the north were the kingdoms of the Picts, with those of the Dál Riata immediately to their west. While it is clear that there were various Pictish sub-kingdoms, it is difficult to establish boundaries between them, other than a general division into northern and southern Picts.

Above: A Pictish silver chain of a kind worn by lords and kings as a signifier of power. It was found at Parkhill, Aberdeenshire.

Opposite: The churchyard stone at Aberlemno features battle scenes. Thought by some to represent the Battle of Dún Nechtain, they may be more generic.

Top: A Pictish overlord followed by two of his warriors, depicted on the stone found at Brough of Birsay, Orkney.

JEWELLERY: STATUS AND SYMBOLS

The Pictish aristocracy demonstrated their power by ownership of extremely fine precious silver objects. One legacy of the Roman influence on the British Isles was the significant amount of silver in circulation. It was easily melted down to create new pieces and, during the 6th and 7th centuries, some of these were engraved with Pictish symbols. In the 8th and 9th centuries, silver continued to be re-formed into large silver-gilt brooches and other items, but none have Pictish symbols as part of their decoration.

Above: A large silver-gilt pennanular brooch, 12cm in diameter and decorated with glass bosses. Brooches of this kind were used to hold a cloak in place, and proclaimed the wearer's status. This example was found at Rogart, Sutherland.

Pictish lordship and kingship was based on power over productive land and men who could fight. The lands had to be protected and, as the opportunity arose, extended. The aristocratic leaders who emerged established strongholds on hilltops or coastal promontories. These were impressive structures, reflecting their occupants' wealth and power. A feasting warband could be accommodated within the high perimeter walls, while the outer annexes included areas for manufacturing bronze and silver jewellery, decorated with enamel, glass and gold. There would also have been stables and kennels. Strongholds by the sea would have had safe harbourages for boats.

Each stronghold, at the centre of an extensive area of farmland, would have been home to an overlord and his kin, along with a household of freedmen and slaves, craftsmen, poets and priests. These centres are seen as larger versions of farmsteads where extended family groups lived, worked and played. Whatever the size of a community, it had to be self-sufficient. Overlords took a share of crops in exchange for protection, but the land could only produce so much. If the population increased, there would have been a strain on resources. Either the lands of others had to be acquired, with new labour to work them, or young adults had to leave.

Whatever the cause, there were frequent periods of upheaval. They may have facilitated the emergence of kings, able to provide greater protection, courts of appeal and opportunities for young men keen to become warriors or craftsmen to a charismatic leader. These kings were the elite of specific kin groups, chosen on the basis of their fathers' lineages.

Versions of Pictish king-lists survive (see page 26) and some of the kings named are corroborated in Irish sources. But understanding such texts is no easy matter. Names and dates can be deceptive. A king may just be named; alternatively he may be called king of Picts, or king of Fortriu – and the location and extent of these kingdoms is the subject of considerable debate, as we shall see. Most of the earliest entries were added several centuries later, to promote an impression of long-lasting power. In certain instances, kings of Dál Riata were added to the Pictish king-list by later generations, to legitimise the Gaelic-speaking kingship of Alba.

THE NORTHERN PICTS

One of the few strongholds that have been partially investigated is the large fort at Burghead. Much of it was destroyed when the fishing village and harbour were built in the early 19th century, but parts of the central citadel are still visible: the massive stone and timber defences around the point of the promontory, now covered in turf; the rock-cut well sited within the lower annexe. A number of small incised slabs, each carved with a bull, were found here during the 19th-century demolition and building works. It has been claimed that around 30 of these bulls were discovered but only six have survived, now held in several museums including the local visitor centre.

It is thought that this fort, situated at a strategic point on the Moray coast, was the power-base for the Pictish kings of the region for over 400 years. It is the largest stronghold north of the Forth and Clyde, facing the all-important highway of the sea. The long, broad, sandy shore immediately to its west forms one of the best harbours on this coast – ideal for beaching boats bearing cargoes or people, from along the coast or across the oceans.

Below: One of the six surviving bull slabs from Burghead.

Bottom: A reconstruction of Burghead fort. This was the northern Picts' most important stronghold.

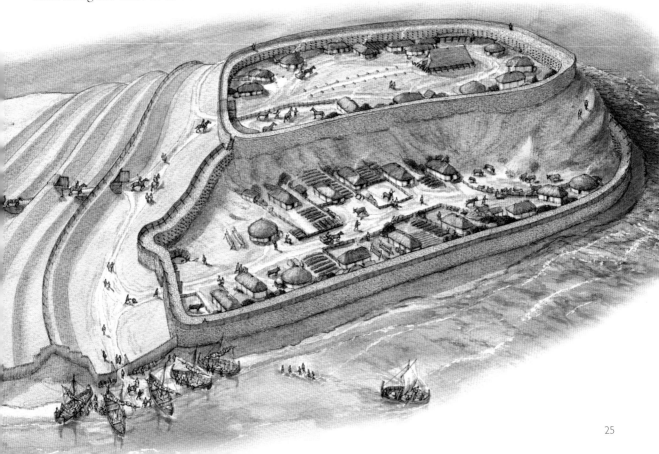

Little is known of Pictish navigation: the only surviving Pictish image of a boat is that on St Orland's Stone near Forfar in Angus. However, the Irish chronicles do provide a glimpse of the importance of sea-going. They record the disastrous loss of 150 Pictish boats in AD 729, somewhere along the Moray coast. It is all too easy to forget the significance of water-borne communications at this time. There were no surfaced roads and the quickest and most efficient way of travel was by sea. This was also of course the only means of transport to and from the isles.

In addition to Burghead, there are a number of Iron-Age forts and smaller defensive sites in the region that could have continued in use during Pictish times. Few of the inland, hilltop sites have been investigated: the stronghold at Rhynie, in a less exposed location, has only recently been discovered.

However, a couple of coastal strongholds have been partially excavated, confirming Pictish associations. To the east of Burghead, investigations have concentrated on two sea-girt promontories by sheltered beaches: Portknockie in Moray and Cullykhan in Aberdeenshire.

Top left: A page from an Irish king-list, incorporating the names of the Pictish kings Gartnait, Drust son of Erp and Talorc. These have been highlighted on the photograph.

Left: St Orland's Stone at Cossans, near Forfar, is unique in its depiction of a Pictish vessel.

Top right: The Pictish hillfort at Craig Phadrig near Inverness.

Both revealed structures of Pictish date. At Portknockie, the burnt remains of the timber-reinforced wall showed how it had been constructed with a frame of vertical and horizontal beams. The structures within the defences included a rectangular building some 4m wide and over 7m long. It may have been a small feasting hall.

West of Burghead, at the northern end of the Great Glen, both Craig Phadrig (near Inverness) and the site of Urquhart Castle have been partially investigated and produced Pictish finds. In Easter Ross, Sutherland and Caithness, an abundance of incised symbol stones has been found, and presumably some of the Iron-Age defensive sites there continued in use. Much further north, excavations at the Brough of Birsay, a tidal island off the Orkney mainland, have revealed a vibrant settlement. It is not clear whether the brough was separate from the mainland in Pictish times, but even if not it would have been an easily defended site. Birsay later became the seat of the Norse earls of Orkney, but buildings from a Pictish settlement have been discovered there. Fragments were also found of a magnificent incised stone with three warriors carrying their shields and spears, as well as two pairs of Pictish symbols.

If Burghead was the main stronghold of the Pictish king of this region, what lands were under his control? Contemporary sources only mention two Pictish kingdoms: Atholl, in the south, and Fortriu, which historians now believe was in the north. Its leadership would have been centred on and around the Moray Firth, where Burghead is strategically sited. At times the power of its leaders potentially stretched from Aberdeenshire in the east to Sutherland in the north and beyond.

The rich farmlands of Moray and Inverness would certainly have been very productive, a major source of wealth and power. The easily accessible sea-ways northwards and eastwards support the idea that this was one of the main kingships of the land. By the mid-8th century a number of Christian sites had been established around the coast. A church known as St Aethan's, presumably a royal chapel, was established within the ramparts at Burghead.

Fragments of sculpted stone indicate that there was a shrine here, with imagery associated with kingship, both religious and secular. During the 8th century, the sub-kings of Shetland and Orkney, as well as those elsewhere, followed the king's lead and embraced Christianity.

The clearest evidence for early contact between Pictish leaders and religious men is the recorded meeting of Bridei son of Mailcon with Columba. This took place at some point between AD 565 and 580. Around this time, lands on the Tarbat peninsula in Easter Ross were given to monks so that a monastery could be established, possibly gifted by Bridei or his successor. From this modest beginning, Portmahomack developed into one of the most significant of the early-Christian sites in the north (see page 49).

We can presume that royal patronage also lay behind the establishment and development of other religious centres at places like Rosemarkie on the Black Isle in Easter Ross (the likely bishopric for Fortriu) and Kinneddar in Moray. Local lords or sub-kings must also have supported the faith. Individual cross-slabs from places like Ulbster in Caithness, Golspie in Sutherland and Dyke near Brodie are surviving markers of early Christian sites, such as we also see at Papil in Shetland and St Boniface's in Orkney.

Above: A Pictish warlord with two followers, as depicted on a symbol stone found at Brough of Birsay, Orkney.

THE SOUTHERN PICTS

The power-base of the southern Picts was focused on the equally rich agricultural lands in Strathearn, Fife and Angus. This is also a region of Pictish strongholds and symbol stones, some free-standing crosses and, above all, Christian cross-slabs.

Fortified sites, like Dundurn at the east end of Loch Earn in Perthshire and Clatchard Craig in north-west Fife, have been investigated and their Pictish associations confirmed. The Irish chronicles mention other power centres and it has been possible to identify where some of them were. These include Dunnottar, just south of modern Stonehaven, and Moncrieffe Hill by the mouth of the Tay. A range of other strongholds have been identified that could be Pictish, but excavations are needed to confirm their date.

'Today Bridei gives battle over his grandfather's land, … Today Oswy's son was slain in battle against iron swords.'

– Raigail of Bangor, 'The Battle of Dún Nechtain', written in Gaelic in the late 7th century

Above: The hillfort site at Clatchard Craig in Fife. Investigation showed that the ramparts around the hilltop were constructed at various times during its 5th to 9th century use. After the first ramparts were destroyed by fire in the 600s, presumably the result of a siege, the fort was re-built with additional outer defences.

THE BATTLE OF DÚN NECHTAIN

During the 650s Oswy, king of the Angles of Northumbria, extended his power and influence both southwards, across Deira and Mercia, and northwards to include the lands of the southern Picts. Irish and Northumbrian chronicles record bloody battles and a few setbacks. But by AD 653 Oswy had won control and established his nephew Talorcan as king of Fife and beyond. He was of aristocratic Anglian and Pictish birth and had been raised among Picts, so he was an ideal placement. After Talorcan's death, other client kings, loyal to Oswy and his successor Ecgfrith, were established in the region.

It wasn't until AD 685 that this Anglian power-base in the north was seriously challenged. Bridei son of Beli had become king of Fortriu in AD 671 and seems to have aspired to become Pictish over-king. In the early 680s, according to the Irish Annals of Tigernach, he 'deleted' the Orkneys and laid siege to the strongholds of Dundurn and Dunnottar. These forts were at the bounds of the lands of the southern Picts, the extremities of the lands and people possibly under the Northumbrian Ecgfrith's authority.

The *Annals of Tigernach* also report that in AD 685, 'Ecgfrith son of Oswy, the Saxon king … was killed with a great body of his soldiers by Bridei son of Beli, king of Fortriu.' This battle marked a turning point. It forced the Northumbrians out of the Pictish territories north of the Tay and Forth. It was also the high watermark in 250 years of Anglian invasion of their neighbours; without this Pictish victory, the modern Scottish border might today be much further north.

There is no record as to where this crucial battle was fought. From the early 19th century it was presumed that it took place around Dunnichen near Aberlemno. However, historians are now suggesting Dunachton by the upper reaches of the River Spey as a more likely location, although we still need to explain the coincidence of the Aberlemno battle scene so close to Dunnichen (see panel).

Before the mid-7th century, monasteries had been established on the Isle of May and at Abernethy, on the south side of the Firth of Tay. However, it wasn't until the late 7th century that royal or aristocratic acceptance of Christianity began to be clearly stated. This commitment was reinforced around AD 710, when Naiton son of Der-Ilei, king of the southern Picts, sought advice from the head of the Northumbrian church. He wanted to ensure that Roman, as opposed to Columban, Christian practices were followed by monks and clerics in his kingdom. He also stated an interest in building a church in the Roman style, which we can interpret as meaning using mortared masonry and constructing arches. Pictish stonemasons had already begun to create cross-slabs carved in relief, as can be seen at Eassie and Glamis, both in Angus. They adopted new techniques of stone-working during the 8th century, possibly influenced by Northumbrian masons.

BATTLE SCENES IN STONE

The cross-slab now displayed in the churchyard at Aberlemno (see page 22) has a series of battle scenes on its reverse face, but how specific are they? It clearly features Picts in combat, one of whom is mounted and may be a king. The other mounted warrior wears an Anglian-style helmet, and may be a Northumbrian king. It was once believed that this was a representation of the Battle of Dún Nechtain in 685, although carved a number of decades later. But, as with hunting scenes on the reverse of other cross-slabs, these battle scenes might best be read as metaphorical rather than factual depictions of historic events.

Below: The cross-slab at Eassie in Angus features an ornately carved cross. The human figure at the left seems to be hunting the animals at the right.

EXERCISING POWER

An impression of how 8th-century Pictish kingships were sustained can be gained from contemporary Northumbrian sources. The kings of the Picts travelled round the countryside with their followers, receiving hospitality from local and regional lords or at their own estates. Craftsmen would have been commissioned to produce sculpture and fine metalwork. Kings presumably emphasised their power by supporting monasteries, linking themselves with the church.

During their travels they could have stayed at these church settlements too.

While visiting, kings would have reinforced their status by meeting with their subjects to strengthen alliances and exercise authority by deciding disputes. Kingly pursuits included hunting, a scene regularly carved on 8th-century cross-slabs. But conflicts were also part of the lifestyle. Raiding and warring remained an essential way of gathering power and riches.

Onuist son of Vurguist was a particularly successful 8th-century king. Coming from the north-east, he fought various regional kings and their warbands to take the Pictish kingship in AD 732. And he didn't stop there. He launched a Pictish invasion of Dál Riata in AD 736, leading an army that laid waste lands and took the stronghold of Dunadd. His brother, Talorcan, was at the head of the army when it overcame the Dál Riatan men further north. The chronicles suggest that Onuist ordered the public execution by drowning of at least two regional kings: another Talorcan, who was king of Atholl in AD 739 and, a few years earlier, Talorc, the king of Kintyre.

Above: A silver-gilt pennanular brooch found at Aldclune, Perthshire, around 6cm in diameter. This would have been a treasured possession of a local overlord.

Above centre: The Dál Riatan fort of Dunadd near Kilmartin, Argyll, captured by the Pictish king Onuist son of Vurguist in 736.

By AD 741 Onuist's power-base included the Gaelic-speaking peoples of Dál Riata. This may mean that he and his immediate followers were bilingual, though we cannot be sure. But, as a result of his triumphs, Onuist must have taken tribute from all who lived north of the Forth and Clyde, and – for a time at least – from the Britons of Dumbarton. His expansionist, often violent, reign lasted for almost 30 years, until his death in AD 761.

Above: The elaborately carved reverse of the Shandwick cross-slab. The central panel includes various scenes, some of which relate to hunting, a pursuit of kings and overlords.

STRUGGLE AND CONQUEST

650s
Oswy, king of Northumbria takes over the southern lands of the Picts. These are held for the Angles of Northumbria until the late 7th century.

EARLY 680s
Bredei son of Beli, king of Fortriu, besieges Dundurn and Dunnottar.

685
Bredei son of Beli leads the Picts to victory over the Angles of Northumbria under Ecgfrith at the Battle of Dún Nechtain.

729
A Pictish fleet of 150 boats is lost off the Moray coast.

732
Onuist son of Vurguist becomes king of Picts. During the following decade he takes Dunadd and Dál Riata. He reigns until 761.

744
Battle between Picts and Britons as Onuist pursues his expansionist policies.

750
Britons defeat Picts at Mugdock, just north of modern Glasgow. Picts suffer heavy losses.

756
Treaty agreed between Picts and Britons.

763-4
The 'Bad Winter' brings terrible weather to the British Isles.

768
Battle in Fortriu between Picts and Dál Riata. Pictish Ciniod overcomes Áed.

THE DUPPLIN CROSS: A PICTISH MASTERPIECE

The Dupplin Cross is the only complete Pictish free-standing cross and one of the most important early-medieval monuments in Britain. At 2.6m, it is also one of the tallest Pictish monuments. Its form and design combine distinctive Irish, Northumbrian and Pictish influences while consciously transmitting an iconic image of royal permanence and authority, for one king and his family in particular.

On the front, a mounted king is surrounded by his armed bodyguard; an inscription on a panel on the back refers to Constantín son of Vurguist. Above the inscription the biblical King David plays his harp and protects his sheep, an allusion to the qualities of good Christian kingship.

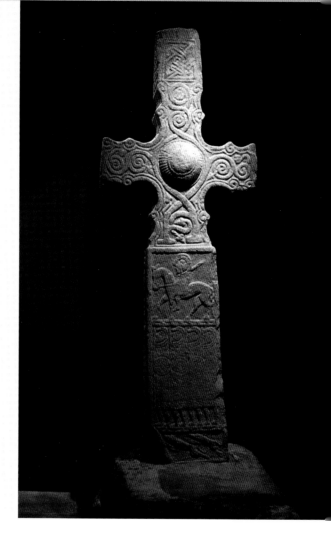

The 'Bad Winter' hit the British Isles in AD 763–4, one of a series of extremely cold, wet periods, resulting in sickness, famine and flood. The impact must have been considerable, since it is mentioned in contemporary texts. Coinciding with the death of Onuist's successor, his brother Bridei, a period of instability followed. For instance, documentary sources record a major battle between Ciniod of the Picts and Áed of the Dál Riatans in AD 768.

While Ciniod won the day, Pictish kingship was by no means stable. Various kings held power between the early 760s and 789 when, after a battle between Picts, Constantín became king and a period of familial continuity ensued.

Most historians no longer think that Constantín was at the head of a Gaelic-speaking Dál Riatan takeover of the Picts.

Instead, Constantín and those who followed him – his brother Onuist, Constantín's son Drest, and Onuist's son Uuen – are now generally accepted as Pictish kings. Indeed, it is suggested that Constantín established his other son Domnall as king of Dál Riata in AD 811. In recent years historians have shaken up all the traditional ideas about the relationship between the Picts and the Dál Riatans in this critical period, as we shall see.

At present the physical evidence for the late 8th and 9th centuries is largely in the form of Pictish sculpture rather than secular or religious settlements. Surviving architectural sculpture opens our eyes to the sophisticated stone churches built under the patronage of kings or overlords: panels and friezes like those surviving from Rosemarkie, Meigle in Perthshire, and Flotta in Orkney might have been used to decorate walls, sub-divide spaces or form furniture, such as an altar. Stone shrines were crafted to contain or cover sacred relics, such as those at St Vigean in Angus and St Andrews in Fife.

The nobility commissioned carved stones to mark their Christian faith and their place in society. These include grave-markers like those from Kirriemuir in Angus as well as the massive tomb-covers at Meigle, St Vigeans and Kincardine in Easter Ross.

Nevertheless, buried archaeological evidence presumably exists at these and other locations. During Constantín's 30 years as king he is said to have founded the church and bishopric at Dunkeld in Perthshire. Either he or his brother also established the royal estate of Forteviot in Strathearn. The core of the estate seems to have been marked by at least three impressive free-standing crosses. Two survive only in part but the third, known as the Dupplin Cross, is complete.

However, Forteviot wasn't just a royal settlement by the river. Constantín's dynasty also commissioned a royal chapel, built of mortared masonry. Nothing survives but the round-arched lintel of an opening – the so-called Forteviot arch. Carved from a single piece of stone, this is the most substantial surviving piece of Pictish architectural sculpture, and indicates an impressive building of considerable ambition. Probably erected within the chapel, it shows a king to the left of a prominent cross and the Agnus Dei (Lamb of God), accompanied by two clerics to the right. They hold staves in their hands, a reference to their marking out a sacred enclosure, in other words, establishing an ecclesiastical foundation.

Above: This carved arch, which spanned an opening about 1.2m wide, is now displayed at the Museum of Scotland. It was part of a royal chapel at Forteviot. It is the most complete architectural element to survive from the Pictish era.

Opposite left: A grave-marker found at Kirriemuir, Angus, shows a hunting scene. The huntsman at the top may represent the deceased overlord, perhaps identified by the symbol at his back.

STRUGGLE AND CONQUEST (CONT)

789
Constantín son of Vurguist becomes king of Picts. He rules for more than 30 years (the start of a 50-year Pictish dynasty).

AFTER 790
Forteviot is established as a lowland royal 'palace'.

793–4
Viking raids begin wreaking destruction in the British Isles.

800s
Norse takeover of Shetland, Orkney, Caithness, Sutherland, the Western Isles, Wester Ross, and southwards into Dál Riata.

811
Domnall son of Constantín becomes king of a reduced Dál Riata.

820
Onuist son of Vurguist succeeds his brother Constantín. Their sons follow, creating a 50-year dynasty until 839.

839
Invasion of Northmen and major defeat of Fortriu and Dál Riata.

842/3
Cinead son of Alpín (known today as Kenneth mac Alpin) becomes king of Picts.

858
Cinead son of Alpín dies at Forteviot. He is succeeded by his brother Domnall and then his sons (a 35-year dynasty).

862
Constantín son of Cinead becomes king of Picts.

'That Cinaed with his hosts is no more brings weeping to every home: no king of his worth under heaven is there, to the bounds of Rome.'

– 'On the death of Cinaed, son of Alpín',
a later-9th-century elegy written in Gaelic

TURMOIL AND EVOLUTION

For 50 years, Constantín's dynasty maintained its strength, although Viking raids, which began around the British Isles in the 790s, took an ever-increasing toll. The resources of Shetland, Orkney and the Hebrides as well as the islands of Dál Riata were easy pickings for them. The lands were raided initially, but settlers eventually followed and Shetland, Orkney, the Outer and Inner Hebrides, Caithness and Sutherland became Norse territories (settled from Norway).

In AD 839 the invaders swept far inland into Pictish territories, changing their tactics to sustained occupation by large armies. At an unknown location, the Northmen defeated a joint army of Picts and Dál Riatans. Both kings, Pictish and Dál Riatan, were killed, together with numerous warriors. This disaster – and the ensuing demands made by the occupying forces – threw Pictish society into turmoil. Constantín's dynasty ended and over the next three years kings came and went until, in 842/3, Cinaed son of Alpín – Kenneth mac Alpin – became king of Picts.

Tradition identifies Cinaed as a Dál Riatan Gaelic-speaking king taking control of the Picts. But nowadays there is a different interpretation. Cinaed's origins are not clear and he could well have been Pictish. What is clear is that later medieval historians retrospectively gave him a Gaelic pedigree because they thought of him as the founder, with only a minor break, of the first royal dynasty in medieval Scotland.

A TOWERING MONUMENT OF BATTLE

Sueno's Stone, on the outskirts of Forres in Moray, is the tallest surviving Pictish monument, standing over 6.5m high, and probably dating to around 900. There are battle scenes covering one side, with foot-soldiers and cavalry; the conquered are shown slain and beheaded. The other side has a cross, filled with fine interlace, giving thanks to God, standing over what may be a representation of a royal inauguration.

Sueno's Stone may originally have been one of a pair of monuments, but if so the other had fallen or been destroyed before the end of the 18th century.

Opposite centre: A drawing of a Viking longship scratched into slate, found at Jarlshof in Shetland.

Politically, one of Cinaed's most important acts was to bring a share of St Columba's relics from Iona to Dunkeld in AD 849. St Columba was seen as the apostle of both the northern Picts and Dál Riata, and by this action Cinaed very publicly gave the 9th-century Columban church his support in the south.

During Cinaed's kingship the Northmen raided his lands as far as Dunkeld. But it seems that Cinaed was responsible for raids as well – he led sorties into Northumbria at least half a dozen times. However, the kingship of his son, another Constantín, was far more troubled. For instance, for three years from AD 866, Fortriu was occupied by Northmen, who took hostages to ensure their safety during their stay.

Constantín's days ended violently in AD 876, a year after he had suffered a major defeat at the hands of the Northmen at the Battle of Dollar in Clackmannanshire. Some regard his death as the end of Pictish kingship. Such was the instability that a couple of years later St Columba's relics were taken from Dunkeld to Ireland for safekeeping. But Fortriu and the Picts do not actually disappear from the documents until the early 10th century.

In 889, following an extremely unsettled period, Domnall restored Cinaed's dynasty. Although the Northmen continued their raids, sometimes staying for months on end, Pictish–Gaelic kingship survived. However, times were changing, new allegiances were being forged, fresh approaches were being taken to landholding and lordship. Social and economic upheavals, as well as raids and invasions, led to the development of an all-powerful Gaelic-speaking dynasty. While this dynasty had its roots in Cinaed, an event in AD 906 marks the most significant milestone in its advance. King Constantín and Bishop Cellach made a vow upon the 'Hill of Belief' (Moot Hill) at Scone, Perthshire, a newly established royal ceremonial centre, that publicly bound kingship and church in a social contract.

STRUGGLE AND CONQUEST (CONT)

866-9 Northmen occupy Fortriu.

875 Northmen massacre Picts at the Battle of Dollar.

876 Constantín son of Cinead slain by Northmen; his brother Áed becomes king.

878-89 Pictish lands fall under Gaelic kingship.

889 Domnall son of Constantín son of Cinead re-establishes Álpin dynasty.

900 Constantín son of Áed son of Cinead succeeds his cousin Domnall.

904 Constantín overcomes the Northmen in battle.

Above: A detail from the reverse of Sueno's Stone shows vanquished enemies being beheaded.

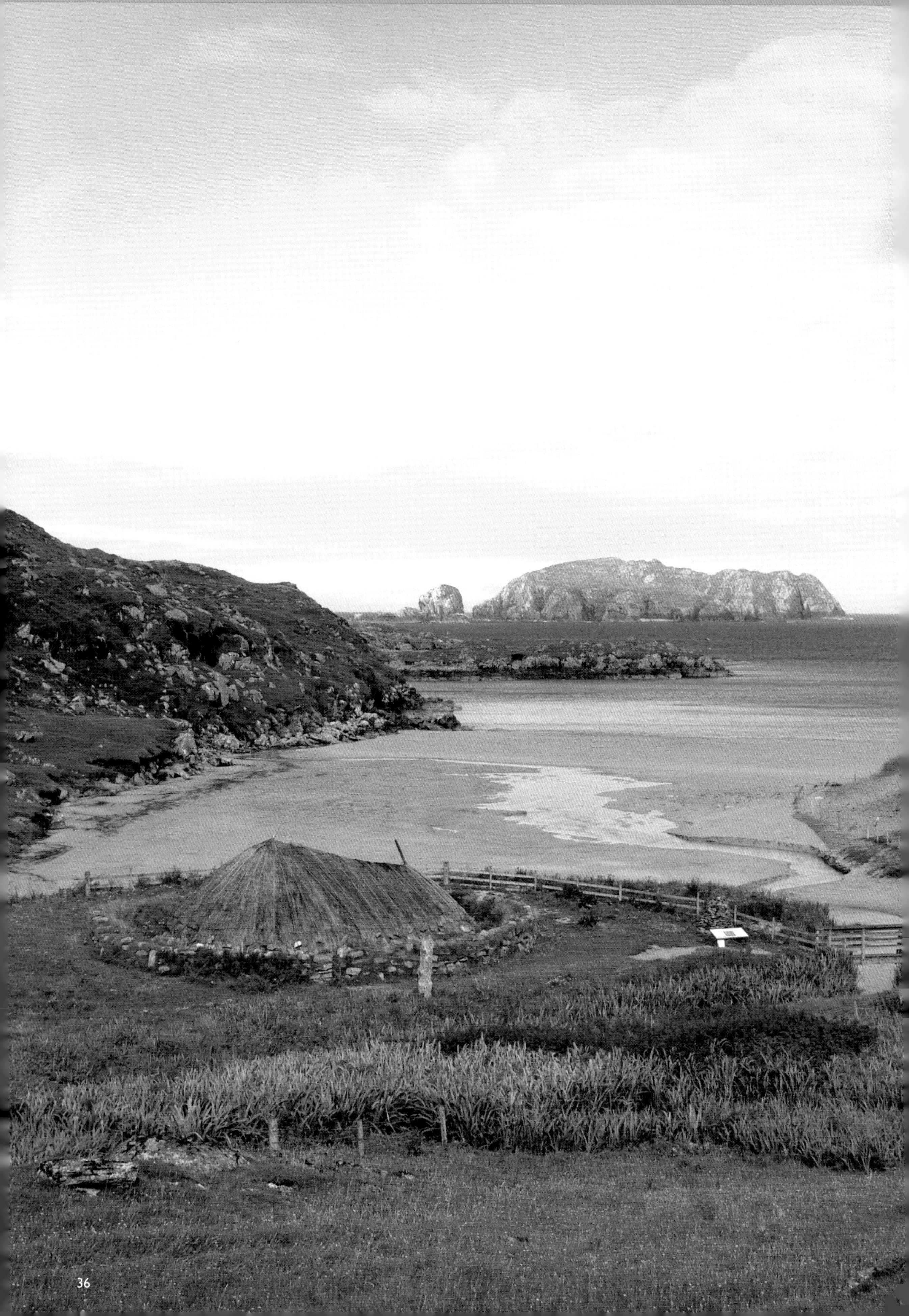

THE PEOPLE

Most Picts were ordinary folk, trying to meet the basic needs of survival – food, warmth and security. They were peasant farmers who were expected to give labour or produce to their powerful kindred, the local or regional overlords. Life was never easy, though – raids, wars and famine often took their toll.

Pictish families must have seen themselves as part of specific kinship communities, whether they lived in individual farmsteads or in small settlements. They raised livestock and grew cereals, fished and hunted. Some people were good at weaving or working leather, others at making tools and containers from wood, clay, bone or stone. Most would have helped to build homes and shelters, make boats and canoes. Some of this has been revealed during investigations at the few Pictish settlements that have been identified, but much has yet to be discovered.

Pictish buildings have often only been discovered by chance, but they reveal much regional variation. Some, in the north and west, have been found while investigating earlier structures associated with the Iron Age, such as brochs or duns, where they showed continuity of occupation but changes in architectural design.

In the east, where the evidence is far less substantial, fewer than half a dozen houses of the period have been excavated.

Orkney, Shetland and the Western Isles have a long tradition of building in stone, either as free-standing walls or as revetments built into the earthy sands, both of which could take the weight of thatched roofs. In these isles, Pictish houses tend to be rounded in overall shape, containing a central large hearth. Sometimes they are two-roomed, like a figure-of-eight. Alternatively they may have a main sub-circular room with several small spaces beyond, which are accessed via short, narrow, low passages. Some areas are paved, particularly at the entrances; others have earth floors.

Opposite: The Pictish house at Bostadh, Great Bernera, Isle of Lewis. The original house was excavated and this reconstruction built nearby in the 1990s.

Top: A Pict portrayed on one of the grave-markers found at Kirriemuir in Angus.

Food was prepared, cooked and eaten around the hearth. Iron knives, wooden boards and clay pots were all used. Perhaps this area was where the occupants undertook domestic work. At other times families must have relaxed, told stories and sung around the firelight. Away from the hearth, there were separate spaces for different functions, such as sleeping or storing food in wicker baskets, pots and textile sacks.

The buildings are surprisingly large, with much the same floor-space as a two-bedroom home today. At Bostadh in Lewis, and Pool and Buckquoy in Orkney, they are set into the sandy ground. Sometimes, the Picts built their farmhouses within the ruins of earlier massive buildings such as the broch at Dun Mhulan (or Vulan) in South Uist. They also built around abandoned earlier buildings, as at Scatness or the Broch of Gurness, Orkney. At the Howe, another reused broch site on Orkney, the Pictish building is rectangular in shape, with rounded ends, a central hearth, and the space against the interior wall partitioned by slabs.

Disappointingly little is known of Pictish houses on the mainland except for a very few sites in Perthshire and Fife. Here the materials used for building are less substantial, with stone for wall-footings, generally turf sods or wattle-and-daub for walls, and large timbers to support the thatched roof.

Long, broad, rectangular buildings with rounded ends, such as that excavated at Pitcarmick in Perthshire, are similar in form to long Highland blackhouses, with living quarters for people at one end and stock at the other. A group of shorter rectangular houses, also with rounded ends, have been revealed sunk into the ground at Easter Kinnear in Fife. These sunken parts may be storage 'cellars' – if so, the houses would have had timber floors covering the space.

These Pictish dwellings were built without windows, so they must have been smoky and gloomy inside. Apart from the fire, there were lamps using tallow or fish-oil, but they would hardly have been sufficient for much detailed work. Domestic activities such as spinning must have often taken place outside.

Left: The child's woollen hood found preserved in peat near Tankerness in Orkney.

Left: The stone-built Pictish settlement at
Dun Mhulan on South Uist in the Outer Hebrides.

Wool could have been spun at any time and any place, and later woven. Everyday tools, baskets, nets and ropes, made from readily available resources, would have been produced at appropriate points in the agricultural year, but iron blades, nails and tools may have been made by travelling smiths. Not all objects were utilitarian: there was jewellery to be aspired to. The ownership of a bronze pin or small brooch would have been an achievement for these peasant farmers. Metalworking of this sort was a highly specialised craft. An unusual example of a workshop has been excavated at Eilean Olabhat on North Uist, the temporary or permanent home of a craft-worker.

Above: A wooden box containing leatherworker's tools, found at Evie in Orkney. Remarkably, it has survived from Pictish times.

Sometimes archaeology provides glimpses of a past that is much the same as life today. Excavations at the settlement of Pool showed that the middens – the rubbish heaps – had been worked over by scavenging cats and dogs. Little has changed there. Occasionally small objects are found that are very personal: graffiti on objects, a playing piece from a long-forgotten childhood or adult game, items that could be charmstones or used for fortune-telling.

One thing is certain, however: this was no idyllic life. Death at childbirth and infant mortality would have been high in today's terms. At times there must also have been shortages of food, or of people to produce it. Appalling winters, like that of AD 763–4, and plagues, mentioned in Irish and Northumbrian chronicles, must have resulted in significant population decline. Like others during this period, the Picts were vulnerable to raids from neighbouring warbands or foreigners. Fear of starvation, slavery or death must have been a constant part of their lives.

For ordinary people, a relationship with their kindred elite was therefore vital. Communities must have given certain goods and services in exchange for the protection of the lord's elite warriors. Some overlords were more successful than others. Thus the people were inextricably linked to an aristocratic society in a state of constant tension and change.

RUNNING A PICTISH FARMSTEAD

All ages would have helped on the farm. Sheep and cattle would have been herded and milked, and cheese was produced. The pigs had to be watched and there was always work in the small fields. The land was manured and ploughed, or turned using spades. Barley and oats were grown, harvested, dried and then ground by hand using stone rotary querns. The resulting flour would be used to make bannocks or porridge. Alternatively the grain was malted for beer.

Herbs and wild plants were gathered for food or to use as remedies. Deer, fish, shellfish, seabirds and eggs were eaten. When animals were slaughtered every part was used – antler, horn and bone for tools; skins for leather. Flax was grown, so linen fabric is a possibility, wool was plucked to weave, horsehair may well have been cut for ropes. Fuel had to be cut and brought in: peat or turf, fallen timber or driftwood.

Left: Timber-built houses at Easter Kinnear in Fife.

TRADITIONAL BELIEFS

Above: The 'cauldron drowning' detail on the Glamis Manse cross-slab.

Opposite: A detail from the largest cross-slab at St Vigeans, apparently showing the sacrifice of a bull.

Top: A figure wearing a wolf mask, depicted on a stone found at Mail in Shetland.

Only a few archaeological excavations have produced any evidence of pre-Christian traditions in the Pictish period. But taken together with knowledge of such traditions elsewhere in the British Isles, they help illuminate some of the rich symbolic legacy of the Picts.

The remarkable consistency of Pictish symbols across a wide geographical area raises the possibility of a priestly caste, or 'druids'. They may have been responsible for the transmission of these designs and, in certain circumstances, for sanctioning their use on stones.

Some of the Christian Pictish monuments depict the most extreme of pagan practices, such as human or animal sacrifice. An image on the front of the largest of the St Vigeans cross-slabs (opposite) seems to show just such a ritual. The crouching figure of an emaciated man laps the blood flowing from a sacrificial ox or bull. A detail from the Glamis Manse cross-slab can be interpreted as an equally horrific scene. It seems to show two human figures drowning in a huge cauldron, with only their legs on view. However, while these scenes may reflect actual pagan practices, their use on Christian monuments is likely to be allegorical.

Particular watery places may have been significant for prehistoric people in Scotland. There is increasing evidence from Iron-Age sites in Orkney, for example, of the importance of complex well structures within settlements. Some of these are central features on sites where settlement continued into Pictish times, such as the Broch of Gurness. They may have provided a medium for making contact with the gods. Rock-cut cisterns are known within the bounds of some Pictish strongholds. While these water tanks were functional, they may also have been used for religious rituals. The most remarkable is the so-called Burghead 'well', where at least one carved stone head is said to have been discovered, a find which echoes the Continental Celtic cult of the head.

There are other examples of places that may have had sacred significance. Between land and sea, on the coastal edge at East Wemyss and at Covesea, the walls of the sandstone caves have been marked with small, roughly pecked Pictish symbols and other motifs. The cave at Covesea had clearly been used for cult purposes in the first millennium BC and later. Numerous human bones survive, with possible evidence for decapitation and deposition within the cave in immediately pre- or very early Pictish times. Excavations on some settlement sites in the north and west have revealed small, above-ground structures interpreted as pagan household shrines.

Some have hearths immediately inside their entrances. It has been suggested that the interior was a mystic space, used by an elite and obscured from the outside by flames or smoke.

Top left and right: Crudely incised symbols found in the East Wemyss Caves in Fife, thought to have been a place of ritual.

Above: The entrance to the subterranean cistern or well at Burghead near Elgin, which may have been used for pagan rituals.

While Christianity eliminated some traditional rituals, others survived the centuries, tolerated or absorbed by the Catholic church. Even now some country-wide festivals hark back to pagan times, such as Samhain – the Celtic new year festival – our Halloween. More exceptional are the fire festivals that have survived in a few places, such as the Burning of the Clavie at Burghead on 11 January – the new year according to the Gregorian calendar.

Second sight, the weaving of 'spells' and the powers associated with certain objects are likely to have been important. Smooth white quartzite pebbles are occasionally found in pre-Christian Pictish contexts, and are presumed to have been charmstones. Even St Columba is said to have used a charmstone, as we'll see. Some small bone objects recovered from Pictish settlements are thought to be associated with divination. The bone piece from Bornais in South Uist, and others from Dun Cuier on Barra, may well have been used in this way. Everyday objects, like beads, pins and dice, can be variously interpreted but some may have had links with the supernatural.

Pictish communal rituals would have needed the guidance of a priest to mediate between the people and the otherworld. A few Pictish carvings may show these powerful individuals – one example may be the 'Rhynie Man'. And contemporary sources do occasionally refer to these priests or druids. For example, their power is recorded by Adomnán, referring to St Columba's magical duel with the magus Broichan.

Top: The Burning of the Clavie, held at Burghead every year on 11 January, thought to be a survival of a pagan fire festival.

Above: A carved bone die found at Bornais, South Uist. It may have been used for divining.

PICTISH BURIALS

After many centuries when little burial evidence is visible, there was a significant change in the early centuries AD. Interment in apparently unmarked graves, or under small stone cairns or earthen mounds, became the norm for some. Certain Pictish men and women were clearly given a ceremonial burial. Although it seems that only a few were honoured in this way, geographically it became a widespread practice. Interestingly, grave goods are rare and there are no visible signs of feasting at the graveside. What happened at a Pictish wake can only be guessed at.

Those who merited a Pictish burial were placed in a rectangular pit where they could be stretched out, usually with the head at the western end. Sometimes there is evidence of a coffin, occasionally consisting of a hollowed-out log, although more usually the corpse was set in a stone box – a cist. In some cases the grave was covered with a small, low mound of stones (a cairn) or earth (a barrow), usually dug from a ditch that marked the site. These ditches are circular or square in plan, the latter having gaps at the corners.

The majority of these ditched graves are only known from cropmarks on aerial photos because the sites are ploughed flat. These are largely confined to the east coast, from Easter Ross to southern Fife, where good cropmark evidence is generally found. Excavations at a few of these sites, such as Redcastle in Angus, prove their date and have yielded some information on who was buried, although no grave-markers had survived.

A few upstanding examples survive in those parts of the north that have not subsequently been cultivated. For instance, at Whitebridge and Garbeg, on either side of Loch Ness, both round and square barrows have been found. A fragment of a Pictish symbol stone – possibly a grave-marker – was recovered from the centre of one of the round cairns at Garbeg.

Above: A reconstruction of a pagan burial showing the body being laid into a stone cist. The grave might subsequently be covered with a low cairn (see page 15).

Some Pictish cairn burials, defined by square, rectangular or circular stone kerbs, have been excavated in the Northern and Western Isles, at Sandwick on Unst and Cille Pheadair on South Uist, as well as on the mainland as far south as Fife, at Lundin Links. The Picardy Stone near Huntly in Aberdeenshire may have been set in one such cairn, though it is almost invisible now. The site was investigated over 100 years ago and, although a grave was found beneath the cairn, the skeleton had not survived.

Individual Pictish burials in long cists, without mounds or cairns over them, are also widespread. They can occur in cemeteries that also contain mounds, or in much larger cemeteries of only long cists. Some of the long-cist burials are pagan, others are not. While many of the large cemeteries are clearly Christian, it is difficult to be certain about other long cists without dating the bones. These graves, without covering mounds, were presumably marked in some way, for the burials often occur in groups and yet respect one another.

The excavation of burials, whatever their form, has produced information on various aspects of Pictish life and death. However, the number of known burials does not include the majority of the population of the period. The invisible pagan dead must have been cremated, sent downriver, or disposed of in other ways, and it is unlikely that anything will ever be known about their lives. But what does clearly emerge is a picture of new and more elaborate forms of burial for the elite, perhaps reflecting a growing aristocracy. This happened at the same time and sometimes possibly in association with the creation of symbol stones. In both we may be seeing ways that individuals and their families asserted claims over land.

Above left: The Picardy Stone near Huntly, Aberdeenshire, featuring a double-disc and Z-rod, a serpent and Z-rod, and a mirror. It may have marked a burial cairn.

Left: This aerial photograph reveals round and square burial mounds at Whitebridge, above the south-east shore of Loch Ness.

ACCEPTING CHRISTIANITY

We cannot be sure how Christianity was spread among the Picts, or how quickly it was accepted. But there can be no doubting the abundance of carved stone cross-slabs as evidence of a new faith vigorously embraced. So how did Christian beliefs make themselves felt in Pictish society?

From the early 4th century onwards, Christianity extended across much of Roman Britain. But the new faith was not adopted by everyone and many remained tied to their pagan rites. Those of the barbarian north, including the Picts, were unaffected by Christian practices. Although the Roman Empire collapsed in the 5th century AD, Christianity did not completely disappear from the southern British Isles. During the 6th and 7th centuries it became more secure on the Continent and gradually spread to all parts of the British Isles.

The lives of some well-known saints native to the British Isles such as Patrick, Kentigern, Ninian and Columba are recorded both historically and archaeologically. The extent of their personal roles in the conversion of the Gaels, Britons and Picts, as opposed to the influence of their followers, is unknown, but the importance of the spiritual and physical foundations they laid is unquestionable.

Above: The 8th-century Monymusk reliquary, the only Pictish reliquary to have survived. It was traditionally linked to St Columba, but this connection now seems unlikely.

Opposite: The magnificently carved cross-slab at Nigg, Easter Ross.

Top: Monks approaching a cross, from a shrine panel found at Papil, Shetland.

HOLY MEN

Colum Cille – St Columba – came across the Irish Sea from Ireland in AD 563. With a small group of followers, he established a monastic settlement on Iona, in Dál Riata. It is thought that the Gaelic-speaking peoples of Dál Riata were largely already Christian, or at least their leaders were; Columba was not entering a foreign land. But that is not to say that all traditional beliefs had been abandoned. They clearly had not. Even St Columba is recorded as using a charmstone. In his 7th-century biography, Adomnán writes: 'From this stream [the River Nesa] he took a white pebble and, showing it to his companions, said to them: "Behold this white pebble by which God will effect the cure of many diseases among this heathen nation."'

Columba must have been aware that the Picts to the north and east of Dál Riata had not accepted the Christian faith. However, Adomnán's account of Columba's life rarely refers to his missionary activities. What he does record is that during one of Columba's travels through the lands of the Picts he met with Bridei son of Mailcon, king of Picts, to negotiate safe passage for his fellow believers. The description suggests that this meeting took place somewhere around the River Ness. The sites of Craig Phadrig and Urquhart Castle are possibilities, as is Burghead, the chief stronghold of Fortriu.

Although the extent of St Columba's missionary work is unclear, it is thought that monks from Iona gradually established small monasteries amongst the Picts. And St Columba was not the only holy man to cross the Irish Sea. One contemporary was Donnán, who tried to establish a community on Eigg in the Inner Hebrides. He and all his followers were murdered there in AD 617. Another was Mo-Luoc, whose monastery was in Dál Riata, on the island of Lismore, Argyll. And around a century later, Máel-Ruba established a monastery further north among the Picts, at Applecross in Wester Ross. Subsequently their saintly lives inspired clerics or aristocratic patrons to commemorate them in various church dedications across the north.

St Columba is simply the best recorded of the influential Irish monks who lived in Dál Riata and beyond. Reverence for saints increased in popularity over time, and we occasionally snatch glimpses of Pictish Christian figureheads in the east. For example, there are mentions of St Ethernan, St Serf and St Drostan, all of whom lived in the 6th century. There are numerous other Irish, British or Pictish saints of this period who are undocumented. We do not know much about their churches or their missionary work. Archaeology could usefully throw light on this.

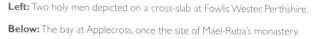

Left: Two holy men depicted on a cross-slab at Fowlis Wester, Perthshire.

Below: The bay at Applecross, once the site of Máel-Ruba's monastery.

PORTMAHOMACK

Archaeological excavations at Portmahomack, on the Tarbat peninsula between the Dornoch and Moray Firths, have certainly illuminated this site. A collection of broken, early-Christian sculptured stones, including part of an extremely fine Latin inscription, was known here. Detailed research has now proved that Portmahomack was a very significant early monastic centre.

Excavations within St Colman's church and beyond its graveyard, begun in the 1990s, have shown that a Christian community was established here, possibly in Columba's time. The area is rich in natural resources, with good agricultural land and a sandy beach providing easy access to the major east-coast sea-lanes. Nearby are woods, wildfowling areas and moorland. This desirable land, virtually an island, was in the heart of pagan Pictish territories. Yet the local overlord, or his king, quite possibly endowed the whole peninsula to the monks to found and support their church.

The excavators found evidence for a religious settlement sited within a large enclosure marked out by a ditch and bank. The community must have supported itself by growing crops and rearing cattle and sheep. Under the later medieval church, the archaeologists found early-Christian graves of elderly monks. A timber church probably existed prior to the sequence of later churches that were revealed. The monks would have followed a strict pattern of worship, with a daily cycle of prayer and readings from the Scriptures. A small bell, a holy book and a simple cup and platter for the sacrament were the main liturgical objects needed.

Left: An 8th or 9th-century iron bell dipped in bronze, of a kind used in Pictish monasteries. It stands about 30cm tall.

Below: Excavations at Portmahomack in the 1990s.

About a century later, towards the end of the 7th century, the site changed dramatically. The monastery developed and prospered as a major centre for craftsmanship, where devotion inspired the creation of texts, sculpture and liturgical objects of decorated metalwork.

Resources, including labourers, craftsmen and perhaps new lands, would have been provided to maintain the monastery. The excavators discovered a large vellum-making workshop, the only known example in the British Isles. Vellum, prepared from animal hides, was used for writing on, long before paper was introduced to Europe. The clear implication, then, is that the monks at Portmahomack were creating illuminated manuscripts. At the perimeter of the site, just inside the enclosure ditch, archaeologists found an area where precious metals and coloured glass were crafted into fine sacred objects within a big timber building. Perhaps also at this time, one or more small stone churches were built, remembered centuries later when the medieval church was dedicated to St Colman. Certainly, a 3m-tall cross-slab was erected that, uniquely, bears a Latin inscription carved in the style of an illuminated manuscript: '… in the name of Jesus Christ the Cross of Christ in memory of Reo … lius …'. It is just one of at least four large Christian monuments at the site, evidenced by the numerous fragments of carved stones found in the excavations.

THE REMARKABLE STORY OF HILTON OF CADBOLL

Since its creation in the later 8th century, the Hilton of Cadboll cross-slab has had a complex and troubled life.

This exceptionally large cross-slab blew over not long after it was erected, breaking off the original tenon – the projecting section at the bottom that was lodged in the ground to hold it upright. The slab was then re-erected, using the lower part of the carved section as a tenon.

On 21 December 1674 a very strong wind blew it over again, breaking the stone and leaving its lower portion in the ground. A local man, Alexander Duff, recognised the possibility of reusing it as a gravestone for himself. His 'barbarous mason' (as the 19th-century geologist and folklorist Hugh Miller put it) hacked off the cross-face and carved an inscription ending '… here lies Alexander Duff and his three wives 1676'.

Antiquarians re-discovered the fallen cross-slab in 1811. A few decades later it was moved to the grounds of Invergordon Castle, on the instructions of the estate owner. In 1921, when the estate was sold, the stone was gifted to the British Museum and transported by train to London. A political and public outcry resulted in its return to Scotland the following year. This massive upper portion is now a key display in the Museum of Scotland in Edinburgh.

The bottom portion of the cross-slab remained hidden in the ground until 2001, when it was recovered by archaeologists. Its burial had ensured exceptional preservation of the finely carved decorations on both its sides and this important discovery enabled a reconstruction of the full height of the slab and its decorative scheme. The lower part of the monument is now on display in the local community hall at Balintore. A replica of the whole stone has been erected at the original site.

Right: A reconstruction of the entire Hilton of Cadboll cross-slab.

It seems likely that the whole of the Tarbat peninsula was Portmahomack's monastic estate, from the narrows at the mouth of the Cromarty Firth to Tarbatness, some 15 miles (25km) to the north. During the 8th century, the monastery apparently arranged the creation and erection of three superbly sculpted cross-slabs around the perimeter of the peninsula. These impressive monuments, up to 3m high and 0.8m wide, survive in near complete form today. The first was positioned at Nigg, by the sea-crossing of the Cromarty Firth, where it is now displayed in the local church (see photograph, page 46). The second was at Shandwick, where it remains in what may be its original position. The third, now displayed at the Museum of Scotland in Edinburgh, was at Hilton of Cadboll, facing the Moray coast, with its major political focus of Burghead 15 miles across the sea to the south-east. Individually and as a group, these three monuments rank alongside the greatest artistic masterpieces of early-medieval Europe.

Above: The cross-slab at Shandwick, which still stands in what may be its original position, though it is now enclosed by a glass case.

Left: An 8th-century Pictish monastery. The church and graveyard are in an enclosure on high ground at the top: the two entrances to the sacred ground are marked with tall cross-slabs. Lower down is a mill-pond, which collects water to drive the mill below. The monastic precinct is enclosed by a vallum – a boundary comprising a ditch and a bank made from the upturned earth. Workshops and homes are clustered around the beach and surrounded by land for growing crops and grazing livestock.

A VERY PICTISH FORM OF CLASSICISM

The St Andrews Sarcophagus is a sculptural masterpiece, heavily influenced by the classical style of Mediterranean art. Its main panel is particularly remarkable. At the right-hand side is a figure identified as the biblical King David overpowering the lion, while in the centre the mounted huntsman may be identified as the king of Picts. This is the most celebrated example of the Picts' use of David imagery (see also the Dupplin Cross, page 32), which they consciously used to link the power of the church with strong kingship, both providing welfare and protection.

Long-standing tradition has established the name by which this monument is known, but it was probably never used as a sarcophagus, or stone coffin.

The panels have now been reconstructed as a box shrine – perhaps created to honour a deceased king – but the pieces do not fit together particularly well. An alternative idea is that they were decorative panels, used to subdivide the interior of a royal chapel. We may never arrive at a more certain interpretation.

Right: The main panel of the St Andrews Sarcophagus.

Not forgetting the now fragmentary monuments from Portmahomack itself, we see here clear evidence for a significant investment of resources. The landscape has been populated with monuments designed to convey important religious messages and social ideals.

Their ambitious design and execution, and the imagery depicted, throw light on the intellectual mindset and artistic influences with which the Picts were engaging.

Left: A fragment of carved cross-slab found at Portmahomack.

OTHER EARLY CHRISTIAN PLACES

There must have been a number of monasteries and church settlements in the lands of the Picts by the middle of the 7th century. Abernethy was established as a monastic site around AD 620. It has an Irish dedication, to St Brigit. Place names, dedications and collections of sculptured stones help suggest the locations of others. Deer in Buchan (Aberdeenshire) is a good example. Its characteristic siting, on a bend in the river, circular graveyard, foundation legend, sculpture, documented extensive estates, royal and noble patronage and 10th-century manuscript all indicate a place of considerable importance that archaeology has yet to confirm.

The best-preserved early-Christian sites are often those in remote places, sometimes set apart from the local population, but these are not necessarily typical of what once existed. An example is the Isle of May, dedicated to St Ethernan, a native Pictish saint. Other sites were even smaller, and harder to access.

Left: The cross-slab by the roadside at Aberlemno. Standing 3m tall, it features both angels and savage beasts.

FOUNDATIONS OF FAITH

● **565-80**
Columba visits Bridei son of Mailcon, king of Picts, probably in the Moray Firth area.

● **LATER 6TH-7TH CENTURIES**
Small monastic sites gradually established in the north and east, including Portmahomack.

● **617**
Donnán martyred on Eigg, in the Inner Hebrides.

● **BEFORE 650**
Monastic sites established at Abernethy, on the south side of the Firth of Tay, and the Isle of May, in the Firth of Forth.

● **672-3**
Máel-Ruba founds a monastic site at Applecross, now in Wester Ross.

● **LATE 600s**
Adomnán, abbot of Iona, writes a biography of St Columba.

● **AFTER 710**
Naiton son of Der-Ilei, king of Picts, acquires knowledge of how to build small masonry churches.

● **731**
Bede, a monk at Jarrow, completes his history of the English people.

● **747**
Túathalán, Abbot of Cénnrigmonaid (modern St Andrews), dies.

● **AROUND 800**
Portmahomack monastery is destroyed by Vikings.

These include Pabbay, at the southern end of the Western Isles, St Kilda out in the North Atlantic, and Rona much further north. Some may have been inhabited only for short periods of time, providing a hermitage for penitents.

Small cross-marked stones found across the country reflect widespread links to the new faith. Some of the stones may have marked devotional sites; others were presumably grave-markers. So simple that they are practically impossible to date, a few may reflect the earlier phases of Christianity but others will relate to later centuries too. Individuals buried in cemeteries now represented a cross-section of society: men, women and children. No longer was formal burial an honour for the few.

Christianity had presumably been accepted by all Pictish leaders by the late 7th or early 8th century. The main indicators of the increasing importance of the church are the cross-slabs that reflect widespread patronage. As public monuments, largely thought to have been erected in the open air, cross-slabs were presumably used during Masses and perhaps as a focus for personal contemplation and prayer. They were large visual markers and, although a significant number have since been moved, many are still associated with later medieval churches or graveyards.

There have been no discoveries of Pictish holy books, leather covers or satchels, wooden carvings or special robes of the 8th century. However, architectural sculpture, such as the Forteviot arch (see page 33) or stone shrines and panels, point to just how much wealth the nobility gave to construct elaborate stone churches, none of which now survive.

Over time, patronage was concentrated on a few major sites, where today we find numerous carved stones – as at St Vigeans and Meigle, or Kinneddar and Rosemarkie. But there is very little written evidence of Pictish monasteries or ecclesiastical centres around this time. One that has survived is a reference to Túathalán, abbot of Cennrígmonaid, (now St Andrews) who died in AD 747. It is not known when that monastery was established. Nevertheless, the famous so-called St Andrews Sarcophagus (see page 52) was probably crafted for a royal patron. It is thought to have been sculpted a decade or so after Túathalán's death, possibly at the behest of Onuist son of Vurguist, who died in 761.

Another key church recorded in historic documents is Dunkeld. Constantín, who was king of Fortriu from 789 to 820, is thought to have established the site around 818. Thirty years later, some of the relics of St Columba were brought from Iona to this church. The rest were taken to Kells in Ireland to protect them from continued Viking raids.

Relics required a container for their safe-keeping. Some are small, portable, house-shaped boxes made with precious metals, coloured glass insets and gold filigree panels (see page 47). The bones of saints might alternatively be kept in shrines. These are heavy stone containers, not designed to be moved from the church where the relics were held. Examples have been found at places like St Ninian's Isle, Burghead, St Vigeans and St Andrews.

Part of a stone shrine was also found at Rosemarkie, along with several sculpted panels made for a church. But this important Christian site is best known for its slim cross-slab, over 2.5m tall but only 0.6m broad, possibly dating from the later 8th century. This is an intricate masterpiece of abstract ornamentation, without figurative or animal art. The crosses on both sides are quite small, in striking contrast to other cross-slabs of the period.

Slabs of a similar shape were produced for other Pictish Christian sites. For instance, the one now at Fowlis Wester in Perthshire stands over 3m high but is only 0.8m wide. But cross-slabs were not the only style of sculpture to be developed. A few masons adapted the forms of Anglian and Irish free-standing crosses. Pictish examples include those at St Vigeans, St Andrews and Dupplin, created in the 9th century.

All of these sculptures, as well as sacred vessels and other liturgical items, reflect both growing self-assurance in craftsmanship and substantial royal and noble patronage. Along with church buildings and estates, they reflect the fact that before the end of the 8th century the relationship between Christianity and Pictish kingship had become a very strong one of mutual dependency, and one that continued to thrive.

Left: The cross-slab found at Rosemarkie, which has lost both its top and its base.

Above: Part of the hoard, now displayed at the Museum of Scotland in Edinburgh.

THE ST NINIAN'S ISLE HOARD

One of the best-known discoveries of Pictish silver occurred in 1958, on the tidal island of St Ninian's Isle, Shetland. It was found during the excavation of an early church site, placed under a small, cross-marked slab in the floor. Originally within a larch box, the hoard consists of eight silver bowls, twelve brooches, a spoon, a sword pommel and two chapes – protective ends for leather scabbards – one of which has a Latin inscription ('*in nomine d. s*' 'in the name of God'). There are also four other silver objects of unknown function, as well as the jawbone of a porpoise. The significance of the jawbone is not known, but the wealth represented by the silver is clear.

The objects are thought to have been hidden around 800, presumably in response to the threat of Viking raids. But who owned them? They are an interesting mix of secular and ecclesiastical objects, some of which were presumably gifts to the church and a possible source of wealth. The bowls could have been used in the Mass, but that may not have been their original function. They are not a set. It seems likely therefore that the items were given to the church at different times and by various wealthy people.

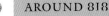

FOUNDATIONS OF FAITH (CONT)

AROUND 818
Constantin establishes the church-settlement and bishopric at Dunkeld.

AROUND 840
Thana works as a scribe at Meigle, a royal church-settlement.

849
St Columba's relics moved from Iona for safe-keeping and divided between Ireland and Dunkeld.

865
Tuathal son of Ártgus, chief bishop of Fortriu and abbot of Dunkeld, dies.

878
St Columba's relics in Dunkeld are taken to join those already in Ireland.

Below: A shrine panel from Papil in Shetland shows five hooded monks approaching a cross.

IMAGES OF FAITH

One of the effects of accepting Christianity was a particularly striking development in Pictish art. Craftsmen quarried stone slabs and carved them with images in relief. The resulting cross-slabs, grave-markers, free-standing crosses, shrine and altar panels are filled with elaborate Christian iconography. They are very accomplished sculptural achievements.

The cross is the principal symbol of Christianity, representing Christ's crucifixion, resurrection and ascension. It therefore occupies a central position on most Pictish Christian sculpture. Some crosses are simple and incised on small slabs or boulders, but many of those carved in relief on large slabs are artistic masterpieces.

The central crossing, arms and shaft are usually filled with curved interlace, geometric key-patterns and spirals, which were presumably designed to aid religious contemplation.

The Eucharist, or Mass, is a fundamental rite of the Christian faith, the consecrated bread and wine representing the last meal of Christ before his crucifixion. A few of the cross-slabs bear witness to this important ritual. On the Nigg cross-slab (see page 46), St Paul and St Antony are shown receiving God's gift of the consecrated host, brought to them in the desert by a raven. A variant can be seen on the largest of the cross-slabs at St Vigeans.

Opposite: Opening page of the Gospel of St Matthew from the *Book of Kells*. Probably produced at Columba's monastery on Iona, this superb illuminated manuscript shows evidence of shared influences.

Right: A cross carved on a small cannel-coal pendant, about 3.5cm wide, found at Beauly, near Inverness.

Top: The Old Testament King David represented as a harpist on the Dupplin Cross.

These images are potent ones, particularly for those who favoured a monastic or hermit's lifestyle, as represented by the two saints. The Eucharist is depicted in other ways too. The carefully executed vine-scroll that forms the borders of the Hilton of Cadboll cross-slab (see pages 11 and 50) symbolises the consecrated wine, which in turn signifies the blood of Christ. The vine-scroll motif is one of the clearest signs of the Pictish church's long-distance connections, for it is much more common on Anglo-Saxon art, itself influenced by Mediterranean culture.

Christian ideas were also expressed in the form of human figures from the Bible. The cross face of the Elgin Cathedral slab incorporates images of the four Evangelists, Matthew, Mark, Luke and John. The Apostles Stone, now in the cathedral at Dunkeld, Perthshire, features two rows of six figures which could represent the 12 disciples. They are certainly depicted on one of the broken slabs excavated at Portmahomack.

But the biblical figure who appears most frequently on Pictish stones is the Old Testament King David – psalmist, prophet and protector of his people. He saved his flock – represented by a ram – from disaster by killing the attacking lion, and is shown rending apart the animal's jaws. Again this is evidence that the Picts were absorbing influences from overseas. David is depicted in an indigenous style of sculpture on the Aberlemno roadside slab, the Dupplin Cross and the Aldbar cross-slab, but the subject matter is inspired by classical examples. And on the St Andrews Sarcophagus, the carving of David is clearly drawing more directly on Mediterranean sources (see page 52).

The use of such a classical style in Pictish art is surprising to some, but fine sacred and secular objects must have been brought to the Pictish lands from the Continent. Kings and their closest kin, as well as some monks, clerics and specialist craftsmen, must have journeyed within the British Isles, perhaps seeing Roman sculptures in places like Carlisle, York and London. Some travelled across Europe, a few to Rome.

Left: The Apostles Stone at Dunkeld Cathedral. Its many indistinct carvings include 12 figures that probably represent Christ's disciples.

Below: A detail of the Aldbar cross-slab shows King David slaying the lion. His harp is at the right, above a ram representing his flock.

They would have seen superb sculptures, manuscripts, ivories and metalwork. Back home, these influences merged with the Picts' own artistic style, as monasteries both produced and cared for some exceptional Christian artefacts.

As a result of these influences, Pictish imagery not only accommodated new motifs; some of its older motifs acquired new meanings. The clearest example is the snake. This had long been one of the most widely used Pictish symbols; now it was incorporated into Christian iconography, with fresh significance. Today, we are familiar with the serpent as a symbol of the Fall: in the book of Genesis, Satan assumes this form to lure Adam and Eve into sin. But in Pictish Christian sculpture the serpent can be interpreted as representing both Christ's resurrection and the rebirth of baptism, symbolised by the shedding of its skin.

Some Pictish sculptors introduced creatures from classical mythology. The centaur on the Glamis Manse stone is a powerful figure – part man, part horse – with an axe in each hand, and yet possibly associated with healing. As we have already seen, hippocamps – part horse, part fish – appear on several cross-slabs. They seem to be benign creatures – an idea supported by their appearance on the grave-cover known as Meigle 26 (see page 61).

By contrast, a sea-monster – the ketos – is a threatening presence, used to show Jonah's deliverance by God from the whale, most clearly on the smaller stone at Fowlis Wester. Other sculpted stones, including the St Andrews Sarcophagus, feature a griffin – part eagle, part lion –representing death and destruction. The power of the griffin is accentuated on other carvings by terminating the tail in another fanged head.

Left: The ketos sea-monster, as depicted at the top of the smaller cross-slab at Fowlis Wester.

Bottom left: The centaur with two axes depicted on the Glamis Manse cross-slab.

Bottom right: The griffin brings death and destruction on the St Andrews Sarcophagus.

Above: A detail of the cross-slab from Woodwrae shows a man-eating beast.

Above: Two men attack each other with axes on the Glamis Manse cross-slab.

Above: Two bird-headed figures on the Papil slab seem to devour a human head.

However, classical creatures on Pictish Christian stones should not be confused with the Picts' own monstrous beasts. Pictish imaginations ran riot when contrasting Christian imagery of salvation with the monstrosities of Hell. Perhaps these bestial images resonated with long-held pagan beliefs. Terrifying creatures often populate the sides of grave-covers; and many cross-slabs are rich with imaginary beasts vying with the cross for dominance. Examples include the Dunfallandy stone (see page 3) and the stone from Woodwrae in Angus (now in the Museum of Scotland). Some of the creatures are shown both attacking and devouring their human or animal prey.

Such images of the terror of Hell and damnation are matched by the inclusion of strange human figures. The combat between the animal-headed individuals on the stone from Murthly in Perthshire is detailed and terrifying. Other figures may appear alarming but interpretations vary. Do they represent feared warrior leaders or characters from Hell? The men in combat on the Glamis Manse stone are fighting with axes.

The figure on the Golspie slab brandishes a knife in one hand and an unusually-shaped axe in the other (see page 7). The two bird-headed individuals on the slab from Papil in Shetland pecking away at a person's head are either pagan priests or agents of evil.

Although much of the Christian imagery on Pictish cross-slabs requires some interpretation, some figures can be identified without any knowledge of Christianity. The bearers of the faith – abbots, monks, bishops or clerics – are immediately recognisable, dressed in their hooded cloaks with crosiers or Bibles in hand. Angels also appear regularly. They are reminders of the strength of Christianity in this world and the next.

The relevance of these images would not have been lost on the people who used the monuments as devotional aids. And for those who had not yet accepted the Christian faith, they would have been impressive indicators of the power of the new religion and its patrons.

DEATH AND SALVATION

The top surface (left) of this massive carved stone grave-cover at Meigle museum is covered with images relating to Christian beliefs. The three serpents coiled and apparently biting each other represent the resurrection. The diagonal cross, representing salvation, has four sets of three bosses within its arms, a reference to the 12 Apostles, the original disciples of Christ. The two hippocamps may be guardians of the faith. Running along the two sides of the stone (below) are representations of life, of the certainty of death, and of Hell.

The monument is incomplete. The open jaws of the opposing creatures at the head of the upper surface are clamped around a gaping recess. An upright cross once stood in this slot, but its imagery has to be left to the imagination.

This is an intellectually challenging masterpiece, wonderfully executed in differing degrees of relief. The overtly Christian top is carved in deep 3D, whereas the sides are less so, and the end is purely two-dimensional. This must be a reinforcement of the Christian message.

GUIDE TO ST VIGEANS

The Christian centre at St Vigeans is an outstanding Pictish site, sacred since at least the 8th century. In the 1870s, fragments of Pictish carved stones were found in the church walls. These, and others found nearby, now form an outstanding collection of carvings in St Vigeans Museum.

The village of St Vigeans is hidden beside the Brothock Burn on the northern outskirts of modern Arbroath. Its small group of houses is dominated by the parish church, set on a conical mound, overlooking cottages, watercourse and railway line. St Vigeans is surrounded by good farmland. It is located only a mile or so from the sea and a beaching place for boats. Nearby, on a coastal promontory, is Maiden Castle, a possible Pictish stronghold.

The remarkable natural mound at St Vigeans must have attracted prehistoric wonder. But nothing is known of any earlier traditions at the site. Instead, it is now renowned for its Pictish Christian associations. Presuming that a small monastic site was established here sometime in the 8th century, it must have been with the patronage of the local aristocracy. Even if there were only a few monks, they would have needed a little land and some resources. As the monastery developed it became a focus for burials, some of which were commemorated with grave-markers showing monks, abbots or Christian followers. The monastery may also have become a focus for pilgrimage.

Vigean (Féchín in Irish Gaelic) was a 7th-century Irish monk who was abbot of Fore in Co Meath. He founded the remote island monastic site of High Island, off the Connemara coast in the far west of Ireland. An early-medieval biography records that he died in AD 664, '… a man of bright, summery life, an abbot and an anchorite, fair-worded Féchín of Fore …'. His commitment to an austere way of life must have captured the imagination of some of his monks, who crossed the seas and travelled through the north of Britain. Or his reputation reached across the Irish Sea and influenced some of the monks who established a few centres of Christian faith. Féchín is not only remembered today in the place name of St Vigeans; his name is also recorded in the early Christian sites of Ecclefechan and Torphichen.

Opposite: The grave-marker St Vigeans 10. About 60cm high and carved on both faces, it has a tenon at its base to hold it upright.

Above: A huntsman with crossbow and a boar from the Drosten Stone.

CROSS-SLABS

The tall, broad, reddish stone (St Vigeans 7) may be the earliest of St Vigeans' cross-slabs, commissioned by a local overlord. It has suffered significant damage, but when first crafted it must have been a striking sight, on the top of the mound, for all to see. It originally stood over 2m high and 1m wide. Its design is distinctive: a Christian cross is carved in relief on both faces, surrounded by human figures and (now lost) hybrid beasts, animals and Pictish symbols.

The two images of the cross are filled with spirals, complex interlace and geometric key-pattern. Unfortunately most of the carving has been removed from one face but the other has survived more or less intact. On either side of the cross-shaft there are various human figures carved in shallow relief. Here there are probably both Christian and pagan designs: two monks, one carrying a satchel that must have held a book or reliquary; St Antony and St Paul seated on thrones receiving bread from a raven; what could be a bull sacrifice; and perhaps the death of a non-believer, depicted upside-down.

The craftsman was obviously influenced by designs commonly used on other Christian artefacts, integrating Irish, Pictish and Anglian styles. The detail of the four spirals is wonderful: one set with interlocked human heads, their pointed noses and goatee beards clearly defined, another with long-snouted beasts grasping each other's throats, the third with what seem to be tadpoles, the last with long-beaked birds centred around a berry. Similar devices appear frequently on the pages of illustrated manuscripts of the period.

Fortunately there are two other nearly complete cross-slabs at St Vigeans. One (St Vigeans 2) would originally have been around 1.4m tall and 0.5m wide but only the cross-shaft survives. A series of Pictish symbols stand proud, if less well-executed, on either side of the decorated shaft.

Right and far right:
The damaged cross-slabs known as St Vigeans 2 and St Vigeans 7, shown to scale. The missing portions have been sketched in to give an idea of their original size and shape.

Left: The front and back of the Drosten Stone.

Above: The inscribed panel at the foot of one side of the Drosten Stone.

THE DROSTEN STONE

The other cross-slab, just as slim, is the Drosten Stone. It stands 1.75m tall but is only 0.55m wide. It dates to the later 8th or 9th century, set up as the focus of this Christian site at the behest of aristocratic overlords. Details on this narrow Pictish cross-slab, carved on all four sides, may have been influenced by a knowledge of certain Irish monuments.

Although no longer complete, the Drosten Stone is a very sophisticated creation, full of Christian and Pictish symbolism. The artistic craftsmanship of the high-relief carving is very fine. The narrowness of the stone demands an elongated cross, which is filled with interlace. The space either side of the cross-shaft features deformed monsters, apparently tamed. Some have their tails interwoven with their legs; one is being flattened against the surface of the stone. Above the left arm of the cross is a small winged figure – full frontal – an impish devil rather than an angel. The left side is filled with refined vine-scrolls. But at the top the sculptor has introduced a wee animal, feasting off the berries. It is a delightful expression of individuality.

The back is filled with naturalistic animals and accomplished symbols. The hunting dog chasing a stag is a Pictish design, although it is usually shown alongside an aristocratic huntsman on horseback. Perhaps here the suggestion of a quest for salvation was sufficient. Below the Pictish symbols is a pastoral scene, including a doe suckling a fawn, a bird of prey – a sea-eagle or an osprey – which has caught a large salmon, and a bear.

But the scene is not entirely tranquil. Even here there is a monstrous beast, a big dog or lion, with enlarged head and horns.

For whatever reason, the carvings on this cross-slab have survived far better than those on the other two at St Vigeans. And one of the most important details can still be seen at the bottom of the right side. Under a frame of interlace is a largely blank panel, the top of which is inscribed in Roman letters. The rest of the area is plain, either because the rest of the text has worn away, or because this was all that was intended:

Drosten ∴•
ipeuoret | ettfor | cus

Scholars suggest various ways of interpreting this inscription of Pictish and Gaelic personal names. But the names are confusing. Do they refer to aristocratic individuals or saints? How did those named relate to each other, or were they connected at all? Could one of the names be that of the craftsman?

Drosten | ipe (or ire) Uoret | ett For | cus
Drosten in the reign of Uoret, and Forcus *or*
St Drosten, the carving of Uoret, and St Forcus

Variations on these translations, and others, are all considered possibilities. The implication is that the stone could have been commissioned in memory of the named aristocrat(s) or saint(s).

Left: The small cross-head, St Vigeans 15. Its shaft has not survived.

FREE-STANDING CROSSES

Most of the sculptured stones at St Vigeans have been re-sized and used in various building phases of the church. But fragments are recorded from at least three free-standing crosses and a 'pillar' cross. Both of these types of monument have an ancestry in the far west of the country. Although carved locally, the pillar cross is a particularly unusual monument for the north of Britain. When found at Irish monasteries, pillar crosses are located at specific points outside the core: by a well or a water-crossing, at an entrance to the monastic lands or the sacred area. The recovery of the pillar cross from St Vigeans reinforces the theory that there was a small monastery here, rather than just a church.

In Ireland and the west of Britain, free-standing crosses were erected beside churches or, like pillar crosses, in early Christian monastic landscapes. However, these are not common monuments in the north-east of Britain.

The pieces from free-standing crosses that have been found at St Vigeans provide further support for the theory that this was indeed a monastic site.

St Vigeans 9 is from a huge free-standing cross, well over 2m high, with a shaft some 0.3m square supporting a massive cross-head around 1m broad. The cross-head that survives of St Vigeans 15 is quite small. Originally, it would have been set on a tall, slender shaft presumably carved with interlace or geometric key-pattern on all four sides. The third was lost over a century ago, but surviving records suggest that it was a small-headed cross, similar to one found at the monastery of Kingarth on the Isle of Bute.

There are two other pieces – both, coincidentally, featuring the Pictish double-disc and Z-rod symbol – which researchers have suggested could also be from free-standing crosses (St Vigeans 5 and 6).

If so, there were once at least five such monuments at St Vigeans – a surprisingly high number when compared to the number of similar surviving monuments at sites like St Andrews.

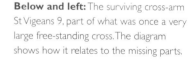

Below and left: The surviving cross-arm St Vigeans 9, part of what was once a very large free-standing cross. The diagram shows how it relates to the missing parts.

Left: The pillar cross, St Vigeans 16.

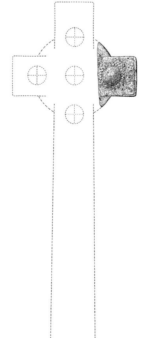

SHRINE

St Vigeans 29, the surviving sliver from a 9th-century solid shrine-shaped stone, is one of the most important fragments. It is also one of the most difficult to envisage as part of a larger whole.

The success of a monastic site at St Vigeans would have depended on continued patronage. Support could have been guaranteed by the transfer of relics from Fore or from one of the larger monasteries associated with St Féchín. The saint's relics – a fragment of clothing or a bone or two from his skeleton – would have been placed in a stone reliquary in the heart of the church. It is possible that this fragment is part of such a shrine.

A carved roof-design, stylistically similar to that on the sliver at St Vigeans, can be seen on a solid shrine-shaped stone found at St Andrews. It is thought to have provided a secure cover for a small tomb, and the St Vigeans shrine may well have been used in a similar way.

Geological work shows that this shrine was carved from the same outcrop of rock as the Drosten Stone, the small cross-head (St Vigeans 15), and one of the grave-covers (St Vigeans 8).

The nearest possible source is 5 miles – 8km – away, so considerable work was involved in quarrying and transporting. It therefore seems likely that a single, possibly royal, patron commissioned all of these sculptures as part of a co-ordinated programme of works, perhaps to mark a particular event, such as the translation of relics to St Vigeans in the 9th century. It is possible that these relics created a focus for pilgrimage, ensuring the importance of this Christian site into the 10th century and beyond.

GRAVE-COVERS

Aristocratic patronage for St Vigeans is not just reflected by its crosses. At least three large grave-covers have been found here (St Vigeans 8, 13 and 14). These are thick, flat slabs, each top surface being carved in relief within a deep decorated frame. Only one still has the slot for its upright cross. Most of the sides have been hacked off, but where they survive they are incised with desperate figures or animals trying to escape monstrous beasts. The message about the threat of damnation is clear.

Top left: St Vigeans 29, the surviving portion of a 'house shrine'.

Top right: The complete 'house shrine' found at St Andrews, across the Firth of Tay from St Vigeans.

Above left: The side of the grave-cover St Vigeans 8.

Left: The top of the grave-cover St Vigeans 14.

GRAVE-MARKERS

At least 10 of the other carved stones found at St Vigeans are grave-markers; and a few are almost complete. On one side there is always a cross, its arms often connected by a ring. It is flanked with interlace, clerics or beasts. The other side may include Pictish symbols, monks, a horse-rider or another cross filled with interlace.

There is quite a variety in these details. One of the nearly complete grave-markers (catalogued in two parts as St Vigeans 12 and 24) has crosses on both faces, each sculpted as if it is set on an arched base. Another (St Vigeans 10) has a blank space to one side of the cross-shaft that could have been used for a carved or painted inscription. St Vigeans 19 is particularly exquisite. On one face is a fragment of filled cross; on the other a delicately carved resting stag.

There appears to be a preference for Christian figures on these grave-markers. St Vigeans 11 has clerics on both sides. On the front a figure is holding a holy book; to the right there is an angel. The back has two seated figures, each holding a book and short staff with a decorative head. St Vigeans 4 and 21 together show a monk on horseback; St Vigeans 7 has a single cleric. This contrasts with the aristocratic horse-riders who appear on the grave-markers from Kirriemuir and Meigle, although there are a couple of less-accomplished versions at St Vigeans. The choice may be linked to the person buried but the carvings also reflect their Christian faith.

Among the grave-markers from St Vigeans there are also three other small, plain stones. Each has a relief cross on one side, but no decoration.

Top row, left to right: The front and back of St Vigeans 11, carved on both sides with human and angelic figures; the front and back of St Vigeans 22 and 23, with a cross on one side and a mounted figure on the other.

Left: A resting stag carved on the reverse of the grave-marker St Vigeans 19.

Above: Two fragments from a grave-marker, St Vigeans 4 and 21. The mounted cleric is probably identified by the crosier and double-disc symbol set behind him.

CATALOGUE

A complete list of the Pictish stones in the St Vigeans collection. The numbering system was devised more than a hundred years ago and should not be considered a guide to the age, style or function of the stones.

1 The Drosten Stone: a tall, slender cross-slab.

2 Part of a tall cross-slab: only the cross with symbols to either side of the shaft survive on one face.

3 Part of a grave-marker: part of a symbol on the one surviving face.

4 & 21 Part of a grave-marker: upper part of cross on the front, monk on horseback, crosier and symbol on back.

5 Part of a free-standing cross(?): shaft with symbols on the surviving face.

6 Part of a free-standing cross(?): upper arm of cross on the front face, symbol on the back.

7 Massive rectangular cross-slab, re-fashioned resulting in an irregular outline.

8 Damaged grave-cover: animals on the surviving side.

9 Side-arm of a massive free-standing cross.

10 Grave-marker: cross on the front, pair of clerics on part of the back, decorated sides.

11 Grave-marker: cross on the front with cleric and angel either side of shaft, two seated clerics and two figures below on the back.

12 & 24 Most of a grave-marker: cross on both faces.

13 Damaged grave-cover: carved top.

14 Grave-cover: carved top and one side.

15 Small cross-head from a slender tall free-standing cross.

16 Damaged 'pillar' cross.

17 Part of a grave-marker: cross on the front with cleric either side of shaft, horse-rider on the back.

18 Part of a grave-marker: cross on the front, cleric on the back.

19 Upper part of a grave-marker: cross on the front, resting stag on the back.

20 Fragment: possibly from a grave-cover.

21 See 4.

22 & 23 Part of a grave-marker: cross on the front, horse-rider on the back.

24 See 12.

25 Unattributable fragment: small horse-rider on surviving face.

26 Lost fragment: small part of a cross on surviving face.

27 Stone finial(?): from an architectural feature(?).

28 Unattributable fragment: carving on the surviving face.

29 A section from a solid stone model of a house shrine: perhaps a heavy cover for a tomb containing relics of a saint.

30 Part of a grave-marker: undecorated cross on one face.

31 Part of a grave-marker: undecorated cross on both faces.

32 Fragment of a taller grave-marker(?): part of a cross-arm on the surviving face.

33 Unattributable fragment: top of one face surviving.

34 Part of a grave-marker: undecorated cross on one face.

The collection also includes eight architectural details dating from a later period. The largest of these is part of a 12th-century carved panel of lozenges and chevrons.

GUIDE TO MEIGLE

Sometime in the 8th century Meigle became a major centre of Pictish Christian worship and burial. The carved stones found here are now displayed in a small museum on the site. They include some of the Picts' most beautiful and distinctive sculptures.

Today, the village of Meigle is an unassuming settlement in the rich arable lands of Strathmore. It lies close to the boundary between modern Perthshire and Angus, on the roads connecting Dundee and Alyth, Perth and Forfar. For most modern travellers, Meigle is on the way to somewhere else, rather than a destination in its own right. Its importance in Pictish times is therefore hard to imagine.

More than a thousand years ago, Meigle's location drew much attention. It was a slight 'island' ridge parallel to the floodplain of the River Isla. This dry land above the watercourse, now over 1km to the north, overlooked the confluences of the Meigle Burn, the Dean Water and the Isla.

A documentary source implies that Meigle was part of a royal estate in the 9th century, under the patronage of the king who is possibly named on the Drosten Stone at St Vigeans. By this time, to judge from the wealth and nature of the

sculpture found here, and the evidence for at least one ornate stone building, Meigle was a major Christian centre. The aristocracy clearly patronised it as a place to bury their dead in fittingly splendid surroundings. Where the aristocracy lived through this period is unknown, although nearby Kinpurney Hill is a possible candidate for an early Pictish stronghold.

It is likely that, from the time of the first sculptures, there was already a church building at Meigle, possibly of timber. Timber buildings could be very sophisticated at this time. It may be no coincidence that the Picts sited this church next to a prehistoric burial mound, perhaps adding prestige to their new religious venture. The medieval parish church that later occupied this site was dedicated to St Peter, an association that may stretch back to Pictish times. Around AD 710 Naiton, king of Picts, introduced changes to the Pictish church that resulted in his acceptance of the supremacy of the church in Rome and St Peter. Was the first stone church founded here as a result of such contacts?

Opposite: The back of Meigle 1, carved with Pictish symbols, human figures and exotic creatures. Prehistoric cup marks are still visible at the foot of the 2m-high slab.

Above: A huntsman or warrior depicted on the grave-marker known as Meigle 3.

TWO CROSS-SLABS

The earliest sculpture at Meigle appears to be
a massive carved slab that the Pictish overlord
of the region decided to commission for all to
see (Meigle 1). When first recorded in 1865,
it was standing close to one of the entrances to
the graveyard and close to the prehistoric mound.
Carved in relief, this monument celebrated the
lord's power and confirmed his link with the new
Christian faith. The patron may have seen similar
cross-slabs, perhaps at Glamis, just a few miles up
the Dean Water. He was certainly influenced by
a cleric or craftsman who had strong ideas on
just how such a monument should be designed.
One face has a Christian cross surrounded by
beasts; the other, pictured on page 70, has Pictish
symbols, horsemen and unusual figures.

The large stone chosen had previously been
used by distant ancestors. Its base is covered in
prehistoric cup marks, made over 4,000 years ago,
which may once have extended over more of its
surface. From this, the mason created a rectangular
slab that stands 2m high and 1m wide. He used the
back face for freehand carvings in slight relief,
removing any ancient cup marks in the process.
Across the top half are confidently carved pairs
of Pictish symbols, large and small.

The lower part includes some unusual images.
Where did the craftsman get his illustrations for a
kneeling camel and broad-winged 'god' or angel?
These are figures from beyond Europe. He may
have marvelled at the very existence of these
creatures on an ivory casket in a monastic treasury
somewhere. Or the cleric may have seen them in
a sacred manuscript.

The five horse-riders crossing from right to
left are more easily understood. They form a
sequence favoured by the Picts, the leading figure
representing the patron. But not all may be as
peaceful as it seems. Are the riders being threatened
by the hybrid beast bottom right, which has strayed
from the other side of the slab, a reference to the
ever-present threat of damnation?

Left: The front face of
Meigle 1, probably the
earliest Pictish stone carved
for this location.

For whatever reason, Meigle increased in
importance through the 8th century. Another
cross-slab was set up in the vicinity, perhaps
marking the extent of the sacred area (Meigle 4).
It is clearly the work of a very accomplished
sculptor. The slab is more slender than the first,
being 2m high and 0.8m wide. It has a rounded
top and both faces are packed with carvings in
similar degrees of relief. Once again the cross is
filled with interlace and surrounded by beasts.
Those in the top quadrants are biting the throats
of the dragons that lie across the head of the cross.

The sculptor seems to have enjoyed the challenge
of interlace, for on the rear of the stone any
spaces between the main figures are filled with
convoluted threads, intertwined serpents or
tangled tails.

Right: The front and back faces of Meigle 4,
packed with intricate carving.

Right: The front and back faces of Meigle 2, which may have stood inside the village's earliest stone church. Tradition has associated the central figure with Arthurian legend, but it actually represents Daniel in the lions' den.

Below: Meigle 22, part of a frieze carved in high relief, once a feature of the church.

A STONE CHURCH

Meigle is one of a growing number of sites where architectural fragments indicate the presence and sophistication of Pictish stone churches, although none now survive. Meigle 22 is a deeply carved piece that was once part of a narrow frieze mounted in a wall of the church. A curled animal fragment carved in deep relief (Meigle 30, not currently on display) may also be from the fabric of the church. Both may have been brightly painted. We might surmise that they belonged in a church or mortuary chapel that could measure perhaps 10m long and 7m wide externally.

AMONG THE WILD BEASTS

The tall, majestic cross-slab (Meigle 2) may have been erected inside the church, as part of an even larger monument. The two protuberances on each side of the slab could have held sculpted panels to the left and right. The resulting structure would have been very impressive. Some have suggested that it formed part of a chancel screen, separating worshippers from celebrants, others that it might have been set up in a private funerary chapel.

A more straightforward interpretation is that this monument stood in the open air, one of a number of fine cross-slabs around the church. These definitely included Meigle 1 and 4 but there are also fragments that could be from at least one other (Meigle 27, 29 and 32).

The central carvings on the back of Meigle 2 represent the salvation of Daniel in the lions' den. But they are also the root of the Arthurian tradition associated with Vanora's Grave – the local name for the mound beside which the stone once stood. In the past, Daniel's long robes have been misinterpreted as those of a woman. The tradition is that this figure represents Vanora, better known as Queen Guinevere, the wife of King Arthur. Late-medieval observers thought that the image showed her death by wild beasts, a fate ordered by Arthur following her entrapment by the legendary Pictish king, Mordred. This reflects the contemporary interest in Arthurian legends and a desire to explain the meaning of the monuments around Meigle Church, including the mound in the graveyard.

GRAVE-COVERS

Meigle also has a striking group of four massive Pictish grave-covers (Meigle 9, 11, 12 and 26 – see page 61 for a fuller discussion of Meigle 26). These huge blocks of stone are known as 'recumbents' because they were originally placed flat to cover the length of a grave. Carved with Christian symbols, human figures, animals and horrendous beasts, these grave-covers are quintessentially Pictish. When first put in place, each recumbent probably had an upright cross-marked stone or timber set in a slot in its top. None of these uprights have survived except, perhaps, Meigle 8 – a fragment of a narrow slab with part of a cross on one side and a pair of confronting beasts on the other. Also disappointing is the fact that only one of the three largest stones retains its original top surface.

Although recumbents are a very unusual type of grave-marker, the artist-craftsmen followed a well-developed design. They were illustrating the pathway from life to death and possible salvation. Two of the stones show mounted figures riding towards the now lost standing cross. All have beasts of torture and combat: a terrifying griffin on Meigle 26 and a pair of bulls almost locking horns on Meigle 12, an appalling contorted four-legged beast on Meigle 9 and a serpent-waving masked human figure on Meigle 11.

Specific details on these 9th-century carvings bear witness to links beyond the Tay. The knot of four naked men on the side of Meigle 26 is similar to the knot of three on a folio of the Book of Kells. The recessed lozenge design across the top of Meigle 12 may have held richly-coloured polished stones. This would have made an eye-catching mosaic of a kind familiar to anyone who has seen the patterned floors of Mediterranean Europe.

Above: The massive grave-cover Meigle 11. The carved figures include an overlord with two followers and a sinister masked figure brandishing entwined serpents.

Below: The grave-cover Meigle 9, with carvings on the side and a slot for an upright in its top.

Opposite top: The front and back faces of four grave-markers (left to right) Meigle 3, Meigle 5, Meigle 7 and Meigle 23.

Opposite bottom right: A reconstruction of the missing panel Meigle 10, with its unique Pictish depiction of a horse and carriage.

GRAVE-MARKERS

A number of grave-markers have been found at Meigle, small versions of the grandiose cross-slabs that once stood here. Although most are broken, there are various forms. Some (including Meigle 3, 6 and 21) are tall and slim, originally standing around 1m high and 0.3m wide. Others are squatter, only 0.7m high but 0.45m wide (Meigle 5 and 23). Many are masterpieces in their own right.

Some of these smaller slabs have Pictish symbols on front, back or side, but others don't. Nevertheless, all bar one reflect a consistent design. A cross in relief fills the height of the stone above ground. It is decorated with angular key-pattern or curved interlace. Where there is space around the cross, it is filled with similar designs, hybrid beasts or figures (Meigle 7 and 28). The other face may be carved with a superbly naturalistic image of a single warlord on horseback (Meigle 3 and 5). Alternatively a vertical sequence of symbols and horse-riders, holy men or other figures may be portrayed (Meigle 6, 7, 14, 20 and 23).

One stone is rather different, being a plain, hollow-armed cross surrounded by a frame of interlace (Meigle 31). The sculptor was obviously working to a pattern and yet, at the same time, was able to express his own expertise and imagination through carvings of varied type and form.

Meigle 5 is carved in particularly deep relief. The front has a frame decorated with interlace. The equal-armed cross is set on a quite unusual base. The upturned animal heads at the corners of the step are amazingly delicate. The horse-rider on the back is placed above a blank panel, perhaps prepared for a painted or carved inscription. A pair of Pictish symbols has been incised on the side of the slab, set apart from the three-dimensionality of this high-quality piece.

Only a few of these grave-markers have survived intact. According to tradition, some were trimmed and set onto Vanora's Grave sometime after the 16th century. However, none of the carved grave-markers recorded in the 19th century were actually found on the mound, except for Meigle 10, the missing panel with its unique Pictish portrayal of a horse-drawn carriage. Most were discovered built into the walls of the late-18th-century church when it was demolished after a disastrous fire in 1869.

OTHER STONES

Over time, people used the stones for other purposes, so many of those on display are fragments. A number were lost in the church fire in 1869, although fortunately the 19th-century antiquarian John Stuart had recorded them first (Meigle 10, 13, 16–19 and 24). Apart from Meigle 10, already noted, they seem to have been small pieces from grave-markers.

Meigle's story does not end at the close of the 9th century. The site was in use into the 10th century and beyond, after the Pictish period had drawn to a close. Grave-markers continued to be produced, such as Meigle 33. One of the later carved stones is massive – a grave-cover of a form known as a

'hogback' (Meigle 25). The carvings on the long sides and sloping end are of roof-tiles, just like those on the hogbacks at Govan, Glasgow. The long ridge is sculpted as a creature with an animal head and a fish tail. The beast seems similar to some of those on the Pictish sculptures at Meigle, a commemoration of that sculptural tradition.

The sculptured stones of Meigle are a fortunate survival from a rich Pictish church, sponsored by a series of powerful overlords or kings. They were able to commission learned men, aware of Pictish, Irish, Anglo-Saxon and European Christian works of art, to produce highly-accomplished sculptured stones.

Below: The late-10th-century 'hogback' grave-cover, Meigle 25.

CATALOGUE

A complete list of stones in the Meigle collection. The numbering system was devised more than a hundred years ago and should not be considered a guide to the age, style or function of the stones.

1 Rectangular cross-slab: probably the first sculptured stone at the site.

2 Tall cross-slab: carved in deep relief on the front, with Daniel in the lions' den on the reverse.

3 Part of a slender grave-marker: cross on the front as well as a symbol; horse-rider on the back.

4 Cross-slab with curved top, packed with relief carvings.

5 Grave-marker: cross on the front, horse-rider on the back, a pair of symbols incised on one side.

6 Part of a slender grave-marker: cross on the front, horse-rider, symbols and hunting dog on the back.

7 Part of a slender grave-marker: cross on the front, symbols on the back.

8 Part of a grave-marker.

9 Damaged grave-cover: carved along its sides.

10 Panel, now missing.

11 Massive grave-cover.

12 Grave-cover with lozenges across its top.

13 Missing fragment: unattributable but with a beast on one face.

14 Part of a grave-marker(?): cross on one face, two figures on the other.

15 Part of a grave-marker: cross on the surviving face with beasts on either side of the shaft. Not currently on display.

16 Missing fragment: unattributable but with a horse-rider on one face.

17 Missing fragment: topmost part of one face of a grave-marker: cross with beasts on either side of the upper arm.

18 Missing fragment: part of one face of a grave-marker: the left arm of the cross.

19 Missing fragment: upper part of one face of a grave-marker with infilled cross arms.

20 Unattributable fragment: carved on one face.

21 Most of a slender grave-marker: cross on one face.

22 Architectural fragment: part of a frieze.

23 Grave-marker: cross on the front, two pairs of intertwined animals on the back.

24 Lost part of a grave-marker: cross with cleric and symbols on the front, cross on the back.

25 Late-10th-century 'hogback', a later style of grave-cover.

26 Grave-cover: magnificently carved on all faces, except for one end.

27 Fragment of a cross-slab: cross on the front, seated figures on the back.

28 Part of a taller, slender grave-marker: cross on the surviving face.

29 Part of a cross-slab(?): clerics on surviving face.

30 Unattributable fragment: carved in deep relief on the surviving face. Not currently on display.

31 Upper part of a grave-marker: cross on the surviving face.

32 Fragment of a cross-slab(?): part of a cross on the surviving face.

33 Part of a grave-marker: later than the others.

34 Unattributable fragment: carved on the surviving face.

Historic Scotland Membership offers fantastic days out all year, plus many other benefits, discounts and special offers.

Membership is available for 12 months or for life, in a variety of different categories.

MEMBERSHIP BENEFITS

- Entry to over 300 Historic Scotland sites as often as you want
- Quarterly membership magazine
- Member discount in Historic Scotland's shops, both online and at individual sites
- Access to over 500 historic sites in the care of English Heritage, Cadw (Wales) and Manx National Heritage (Isle of Man)

HOW TO JOIN

There are four ways you can obtain more information or start your membership:

In person: At any staffed Historic Scotland site or property.

By phone: Call +44(0)131 668 8999 with your credit/debit card details.

Online: www.historicenvironment.scot/membership

By post to: Historic Scotland Membership, Longmore House, Salisbury Place, Edinburgh EH9 1SH.

EXPLORER PASS

For visitors to Scotland, the Explorer Pass offers admission to all Historic Scotland properties for 3 or 7 days. Ask for details and prices at any Historic Scotland property or visit our website at www.historicenvironment.scot/explorer

FURTHER READING AND CREDITS

Adomnán, *Life of Saint Columba* (7th century)

J.R. Allen & J. Anderson, *The Early Christian Monuments of Scotland* (1903)

Bede, *Ecclesiastical History of the English People* (8th century)

M. Carver, *Portmahomack – Monastery of the Picts* (2008)

K. Forsyth, *Language in Pictland* (1997)

S. Foster, *Picts, Gaels and Scots* (2004)

S. Foster (ed), *The St Andrews Sarcophagus: A Pictish Masterpiece and its International Connections* (1998)

RCAHMS, *The Pictish Symbol Stones of Scotland* (2008)

J.E. Fraser, *From Caledonia to Pictland – Scotland to 795* (2009)

G. & I. Henderson, *The Art of the Picts* (2004)

H.F. James, I. Henderson & S.M. Foster, *A Fragmented Masterpiece: Recovering the Biography of the Hilton of Cadboll Pictish Cross-Slab* (2008)

A. Ritchie, I. G. Scott & T. E. Gray, *People of Early Scotland* (2006)

A. Woolf, *From Pictland to Alba 789–1070* (2007)

Specific chapters in:

I. Armit, *The Archaeology of Skye and the Western Isles* (1996)

J. Downes and A. Ritchie (eds), *Sea Change – Orkney and Northern Europe in the Later Iron Age, AD 300–800* (2003)

A. Dunwell & I. Ralston, *Archaeology and Early History of Angus* (2008)

M. Parker Pearson, N. Sharples & J. Symonds, *South Uist – Archaeology and History of a Hebridean Island* (2004)

J. Wormald (ed), *Scotland: A History* (2005)

First published by Historic Scotland 2010
This edition published 2017
Printed from sustainable materials 2017
© HES 2017
ISBN 978-1-84917-034-5

Editor: Andrew Burnet
Design: Contagious UK Ltd
Photography: Historic Environment Scotland Photo Unit
Illustrations pp.1, 4, 7, 19, 23, 37, 41, 47, 57, 63 and 71: Willie Rodger
Illustrations pp.8, 11, 50, 66 and 75: Ian G. Scott
Illustrations pp.15, 38 and 44: David Simon
Illustrations pp.25 and 51: Stephen Conlin/Pictu Ltd
Illustration p.39: Chris Brown
Translations of early-medieval poetry, pp.28 and 34 are reproduced by kind permission of Prof Thomas Clancy.

www.historicenvironment.scot

This guide includes selected places to visit under three headings:

- Individual stones referred to in the text (some have been omitted due to access problems)

- Museums and institutions holding Pictish stones and other artefacts

- Other sites with Pictish connections

An admission charge is payable at sites marked (£)

Information on all Pictish stones can be found on the Canmore website: **canmore.org.uk**

INDIVIDUAL STONES

1 Aberlemno stones
In Aberlemno, NE of Forfar, Angus
OS: NO 522 559–NO 522 555

Four sculpted stones: symbol-bearing cross-slab with battle scene in churchyard; three stones nearby beside the B9134, one with almost invisible symbols. The stones are boxed in for winter.

2 Abernethy round-tower
In Abernethy, just east of Bridge of Earn, Perth & Kinross
OS: NO 192 163

Site of an early Pictish monastery. The medieval round-tower has a Pictish symbol stone set against its base.

3 Aldbar cross-slab
In Brechin Cathedral, Brechin, Angus
Tel: 01356 629 360
OS: NO 596 600

A cross-slab found at Aldbar, featuring human and animal figures including King David and the lion. Also Brechin's Mary Stone, part of a 9th/10th-century sculpted cross-slab.

4 Apostles Stone
Inside the chapter house at Dunkeld Cathedral, Perth & Kinross
OS: NO 023 426

Part of a thick-set stone with 12 figures possibly representing the disciples of Christ.

5 Brandsbutt stone
On the NW outskirts of Inverurie, Aberdeenshire
OS: NJ 759 224

Massive Pictish symbol stone with clear ogham inscription across its main face.

6 Brough of Birsay
On a tidal island at Birsay, 25 miles (40km) NW of Kirkwall, Orkney
Tel: 01856 841 815.
OS: HY 239 285

Pictish settlement, though most of the visible structural remains are Norse or later. Includes a replica of the Pictish stone found here. (£)

7 Clach Biorach stone
Edderton, NW of Tain, Easter Ross
OS: NH 708 851

Standing stone with incised Pictish symbols, probably in original position.

8 Dunfallandy stone
On western outskirts of Pitlochry, Perth & Kinross
OS: NN 946 565

Symbol-bearing cross-slab beside church.

9 Dunnichen stone
Three miles (4km) east of Forfar, Angus
OS: NO 516 496

Replica of symbol stone erected to commemorate the possible site of a battle (original now in Meffan Museum, Forfar).

10 Dupplin Cross
In St Serf's Church, Dunning, 12 miles (18km) SW of Perth
OS: NO 018 144

Superb free-standing cross carved for the Pictish royal estate of Forteviot.

11 Dyce stones
Fergus's Church, Dyce, near Aberdeen
OS: NJ 875 154

Shelter within ruined church houses collection of Pictish stones.

12 Eagle Stone
Strathpeffer, near Dingwall, Easter Ross
OS: NH 484 585

Symbol stone on eastern outskirts of village.

13 Eassie cross-slab
In the old church of Eassie, 2 miles (3km) west of Glamis, Angus
OS: NO 352 474

Symbol-bearing cross-slab in shelter within ruins of church.

14 Elgin cross-slab
At Elgin Cathedral, Elgin, Moray
Tel: 01343 547 171
OS: NJ 221 630

Symbol-bearing cross-slab found by St Giles Church stands in the ruins of the cathedral. (£)

15 Farr cross-slab
In graveyard around Strathnaver Museum, Bettyhill, Sutherland
OS: NC 714 622

Sculpted stone carved with a cross on one side.

16 Fowlis Wester stones
Fowlis Wester, 5 miles (8km) east of Crieff, Perthshire
OS: NN 927 240

Replica of symbol-bearing cross-slab in centre of village; original now moved into church, alongside a second slab found built into church fabric.

17 Glamis Manse stone
Glamis, Angus
OS: NO 386 468

Early cross-slab with large inscribed symbols on reverse.

18 Hilton of Cadboll cross-slab
Hilton, 6 miles (10km) SE of Tain, Easter Ross
OS: NH 873 768

A modern replica near the spot where the slab was found. Most of the original is displayed in the Museum of Scotland, Edinburgh.

19 Knocknagael Boar Stone
Highland Council Headquarters, Glenurquhart Road, Inverness
OS: NH 662 447

Symbol stone from outskirts of Inverness now in glass-fronted reception area of council chamber.

20 Logierait stones
In the kirkyard at Logierait, south of Pitlochry, Perth & Kinross
OS: NN 968 520

Two small cross-slabs, each with symbols on reverse.

21 Maiden Stone
Chapel of Garioch, 5 miles (8km) NW of Inverurie, Aberdeenshire
OS: NJ 703 247

Impressive symbol-bearing cross-slab.

22 Nigg cross-slab
Nigg Church, 7 miles (10km) south of Tain, Easter Ross
OS: NH 804 717

Superb symbol-bearing cross-slab.

23 Picardy stone
Near Insch, 10 miles (16km) south of Huntly, Aberdeenshire
OS: NJ 609 302

Symbol-incised stone in its original position.

24 Rhynie Man
Aberdeenshire Council offices, Westburn Road, Aberdeen
OS: NJ 911 069

Grimacing, axe-wielding man incised on a stone ploughed up at Rhynie in 1978.

25 Rhynie symbol stones
Old Churchyard, Rhynie, near Alford, Aberdeenshire
OS: NJ 499 264

Shelter at edge of car-park houses three symbol stones. A fourth, the Craw Stane, stands in the field above.

26 Rodney Stone
Grounds of Brodie Castle,
west of Forres, Moray
OS: NH 982 576

A fine symbol-bearing
cross-slab.

27 St Orland's Stone
Near Kirriemuir, Angus,
a long walk from the A928
OS: NO 400 500

Rare depiction of a boat on
symbol-bearing cross-slab.

28 Shandwick cross-slab
Above the village of Shandwick,
6 miles (10km) SE of Tain,
Easter Ross
OS: NH 855 747

Large symbol-bearing cross-slab
housed in glass shelter.

29 Strathmiglo stone
Outside the churchyard
at Strathmiglo, near
Auchtermuchty, Fife
OS: NO 209 101

Symbol stone re-used
as a gatepost pillar.

30 Sueno's Stone
On eastern outskirts of
Forres, Moray.
OS: NJ 046 595

The tallest sculpted stone
in Scotland, displayed in glass
shelter; includes unusual
battle imagery.

MUSEUMS AND INSTITUTIONS
31 Caithness Horizons
High Street, Thurso, Caithness.
Tel: 01847 896 508
OS: ND 118 685

Pictish symbol-bearing cross-
slabs from Ulbster and Halkirk.

32 Dunrobin Castle Museum
Just NE of Golspie, Sutherland.
Tel: 01408 633 177
OS: NC 852 008

Outstanding collection of
18 Pictish stones. Closed
for winter. (£)

33 Elgin Museum
High Street, Elgin, Moray
Tel: 01343 543 675
OS: NJ 218 628

Pictish collection includes two
of the six surviving carved bulls
that once adorned Burghead
fort and early-Christian stones
found at Kinneddar.

34 Groam House Museum
High Street, Rosemarkie,
Black Isle, Easter Ross
Tel: 01381 620 961
OS: NH 736 576

Important collection of Pictish
Christian stones includes
impressive symbol-bearing
cross-slab. Closed 1 January
to 5 March.

35 Headland Trust Visitor Centre
Grant Street, Burghead, Moray
Tel: 01343 835518
OS: NJ 110 691

Within the remains of the
Pictish fort. Has two of the
six surviving carved bulls
that were found here.

36 Inverness Museum and Art Gallery
Castle Wynd, Inverness
Tel: 01463 237114
OS: NH 666 451

Important collection of Pictish
symbol stones including the
Ardross wolfstone, and a Pictish
carved cannel-coal pendant.

37 McManus Galleries
Albert Square, Dundee
Tel: 01382 432 350
OS: NO 402 304

Recently refurbished museum
includes important Pictish stones
including Benvie and a
reconstructed long-cist burial
from Lundin Links.

38 Meffan Institute
West High Street, Forfar, Angus
Tel: 01307 464 123
OS: NO 462 505

Collection includes important
Pictish stones from Kirriemuir
and elsewhere in the
surrounding area.

39 Meigle Museum
In Meigle, near Glamis,
Perth & Kinross
Tel: 01828 640 612
OS: NO 287 445

Contains one of the most
notable collections of early-
historic sculpted stones in
western Europe, all from this
Pictish church-settlement site.
Closed for winter. (£)

40 Museum of Scotland
Chambers Street, Edinburgh
Tel: 0131 225 7534
OS: NT 258 733

The national collection. Includes
the Bullion Stone, Hilton of
Cadboll slab, Tarbat inscription,
Forteviot arch, and superb
examples of Pictish jewellery.

41 Orkney Museum
Broad Street, Kirkwall
Tel: 01856 873 191
OS: HY 448 108

Includes finds from Pictish sites:
the Brough of Birsay, Pool, Howe,
Buckquoy, Skaill in Deerness and
various Pictish stones.

42 Perth Museum and Art Galleries
George Street, Perth
Tel: 01738 632 488
OS: NO 119 237

Sculpted stones from Inchrya,
Gellyburn, St Madoes and
New Scone.

43 St Andrews Cathedral Museum
St Andrews, Fife
Tel: 01334 472563
OS: NO 513 166

A large collection of Pictish and
later carved stones, including the
St Andrews Sarcophagus. (£)

44 St Vigeans Sculptured Stones Museum
St Vigeans, near Arbroath, Angus,
Tel: 01241 433 739.
OS: NO 638 429

Recently redisplayed collection
of one of the most notable
assemblages of early historic
sculpture in western Europe.
Includes the Drosten Stone. (£)

45 Shetland Museum
Hay's Dock, Lerwick
Tel: 01595 695 057
OS: HU 472 417

Includes sculpted stones from
Papil and Mail and replicas of
St Ninian's Isle treasure.

46 Tarbat Discovery Centre
Portmahomack, east of Tain,
Easter Ross
Tel: 01862 871 351
OS: NH 914 840

Telling the story of this
important Pictish monastery
from recent excavation
discoveries. Closed for winter. (£)

OTHER SITES TO VISIT
47 Bostadh Reconstructed House
Great Bernera, Lewis,
Outer Hebrides
OS: NB 137 400

Reconstructed by archaeologists
based on Pictish remains found
here in the 1990s.

48 Broch of Gurness
Aikerness, 16 miles (26km)
north of Kirkwall, Orkney
Tel: 01856 751 414
OS: HY 381 268

Ruins of Pictish house, rebuilt
alongside the prehistoric
remains it once covered. Site
museum includes symbol-incised
stone. Closed for winter. (£)

49 Burghead Well
King Street, Burghead, 10 miles
(15km) NW of Elgin, Moray
OS: NJ 110 691

On the site of Burghead Pictish
fort, this rock-cut cistern may
have had a variety of uses,
including providing a water
supply. Access via local
keyholder.

50 Craig Phadrig
Two miles (2.5km) SW
of Inverness
OS: NH 639 452

Iron-Age hilltop fort with
surviving ramparts and evidence
of Pictish use.

51 Dundurn
Near St Fillans, Perth & Kinross
OS: NN 708 232

Pictish hilltop fort site.

52 Scatness
Near Sumburgh, Shetland
OS: HU 389 106

Extensive ruins dating from the
Bronze Age to medieval times.
Excavations are ongoing,
and there is a visitor centre.